The Cries of Men

The Cries of Men

✦

Voices of Jamaican Men who have been Raped and Sexually Abused

O'Brien Dennis

iUniverse, Inc.
New York Lincoln Shanghai

The Cries of Men
Voices of Jamaican Men who have been Raped and Sexually Abused

Copyright © 2005 by Dennis Tyson

All rights reserved. No part of this book may be used or reproduced by any means, graphic, electronic, or mechanical, including photocopying, recording, taping or by any information storage retrieval system without the written permission of the publisher except in the case of brief quotations embodied in critical articles and reviews.

iUniverse books may be ordered through booksellers or by contacting:

iUniverse
2021 Pine Lake Road, Suite 100
Lincoln, NE 68512
www.iuniverse.com
1-800-Authors (1-800-288-4677)

The names used in the book are all fictitious apart from my name and the stories and experiences are all true.

The book is written in the emotional language of the writer. The journal entries are recorded as written in the journal and not free of grammatical or spelling errors. The personal stories are also written in the emotional language of the victims.

ISBN-13: 978-0-595-34139-9 (pbk)
ISBN-13: 978-0-595-78914-6 (ebk)
ISBN-10: 0-595-34139-X (pbk)
ISBN-10: 0-595-78914-5 (ebk)

Printed in the United States of America

To my Grandmother for the strength and love she gave me

To Oprah, who has shaped my life and given me hope! Thank you for opening your world to me, showing me that in this huge world we are not alone. Your courage and confidence has given me renewed strength to live each day. It was your story that inspired me to tell mine. This book has been the best thing I have ever attempted in my life and I owe it all to you. You have taught me how to create my own happiness and make it my choice.

—O'Brien Dennis

The way to choose happiness is to follow what is right and real and the truth for you. You can never be happy living someone else's dream. Live your own and you will for sure know the meaning of happiness.
—**O**prah Winfrey

Contents

Introduction 1
Sweet Sweet Jamaica
   ***Child Sexual Abuse Cases in Jamaica 8

Part I   Sexual terms

Chapter 1	Confession. 17
Chapter 2	Ne Me Quite Pas. 26
Chapter 3	Love Wouldn't Count Me Out 34
Chapter 4	A thin line between love and hate 40
Chapter 5	Till Shiloh. 48
Chapter 6	Men in pain. 55
Chapter 7	Chi Chi Man. 66
Chapter 8	Waiting to Exhale 79
Chapter 9	No woman no Cry 91
Chapter 10	Get Up stand up 97
Chapter 11	The real deal 104
Chapter 12	I Don't Wanna Cry. 112

Part II   Changes

Chapter 13	Truth Hurts 121

Chapter 14	Street Boys	128
Chapter 15	Confusion	135
Chapter 16	Fire pan Rome The Christian Religion and Denomination	147
Chapter 17	Seeking help	158
Chapter 18	Sexual abuse and the family	172
Chapter 19	Why do we trust?	178
Chapter 20	Forgiveness	192

Resources 201
Bibliography 209

Acknowledgement

I give thanks to God for waking me up each day and giving me hope. I thank my mother who as time goes by is breaking the barrier between the both of us. To my sisters, Keri-Celia and Tracy, thanks for your love and support. To my brother André for always having my back. Aunty Vicky thank you for believing in me and giving me a hug when I needed it the most. To my cousin and one of my dearest friend Kamar who over the years, have shown me unconditional love.

Special thanks to the library staff of the W.D. Du Bois Library at the University of Massachusetts, The Brooklyn Public Library and the Mt. Vernon Public Library. This book could not have been possible if it were not for the heartening words and the steadfastness in believing that I could do it. Thank you Colin Channer and thanks to Robin D. Stone who encouraged me to tell my story.

To the five men in my life, you have all asked to not have your names listed, but you all know your abbreviations (Th.Ch.Ta.Co.St) thanks for your friendship, trust, love and support. When I had nowhere to live, you gave me a home, when my family turned their backs I could always count on you all. No one in the world could ask for better friends than you guys. It is your push and bickering words that have led me this far. Th. you are my youngest friend and you are a gem. You have shown me that age is just a number; you have a soul of an angel sent from God. Ch. you have been my conscience, my critic, my judge and most of all a good friend. Remember friends may walk in and out of your life but true friendships last a lifetime. Ta. we have so much in common, you have my drive and my will to break any barrier. Summer 2004 was the best; we did it all! Thanks for giving me back a part of me I thought was lost. St. no words can describe how much you mean to me. You have given so much to have me in your life and I thank you so much. We may be miles apart but your spirit lingers with me everyday.

Thank you Rachel Krupicka and the production team at Iuniverse for their guidance and support. Even though I had a limited budget you were willing to work with me and make this work what it is today.

I am totally grateful to everyone who has helped in giving me their time, space, love and confidence in writing this book, special thanks to the young men who have given their stories to making this book possible. Some of you may not be at the stage to accept the reality that you were sexually abused or even ready to confront your family, but remember in the end true happiness comes only from within. Berry, from day one I could always count on you and you have never failed me. Thanks for your support all these years. Alic Payne Francis, you mean the world to me. You have brought so many change in my life and have shown me a world of love. How can I forget the cold winter nights when I was in need and I could always count on you? Your heart is as warm and bright as the sun. Kevin thanks for your help and counsel and for always talking to me even at the last call. Medrano, I loved you then and I love you now. We both have two different life paths, but you have taught me one thing, life is not what it seems from the outside "nuff respect!" Hey, and thanks for introducing me to Nina Simone.

To my best friend, thank you for opening up your home to me and for giving me unconditional support. You have guided me this far and without you all of this could not have been possible. You have kept me away from a life of destruction. And even though I told you how much I hated you, you were always persistent. God has placed you in my life for a reason, you are more than just a friend you are a precious gift from God.

Introduction

Sweet Sweet Jamaica

Have you ever been in love? And I mean really in love to the point where you feel a knotting inside of your stomach giving you a sense of excitement. The love I am talking about is summer's love. Going far away into the countryside and in the last few days of your trip, you meet someone and your world is rocked. You know it will not last because you are both from separate worlds, yet it feels as if it could last forever. Have you ever loved someone, you would do anything to make them understand? Have you ever had someone steal your heart away you would give anything to make yourself feel safe? Have you ever needed someone so bad you can't sleep at nights words cannot even explain how you feel? Most of my summers were like that and that is how I come to believe in love, and even though love can be painful at times, I enjoyed it for the moment. It is this love that forces a young child, a young man to trust another. Love has a dark side to it and it is this emotional perversion of passion that forces someone to hurt an innocent child or someone close to them.

When I had approached E. Lynn Harris in summer 2003 about writing this book and what advice he could give me, all he said was to write from the heart. The author of *No Secrets No Lies* Robin D. Stone told me that the healing starts only when you have acknowledged that the rape was not your fault. I write only from inspiration. Chapter 1 was as a result of a long weekend of passionate sex with someone I knew could never be mine, as he was already involved with someone else. It was so intriguing and even though we both knew it could never last we took the time to know each other for who we were and making that spiritual connection, only for the moment. The memories of that weekend lingered in my mind for a long time.

I awoke this morning to the sound of rain beating on my windowsill and I could smell the freshness of the air in late July. I wish I had someone in bed with me to share this moment, but I relaxed my mind by watching *Bend it like Beckham* and I was inspired by love. One of the Indian guys in the movie was gay and in love and because of his culture, he had to suppress his feelings. He was willing to sacrifice his desires to love for the cultural beliefs of his family. It is odd how culture at times can force us to live miserable lives. Culture is the values, attitudes and norms of any given society that is taught and learned that defines what is socially acceptable. There is no right or wrong to culture. It's a belief system that changes over a period of time as society advances, both technologically and economically. I once lived in Jamaica, an island paradise, I called home and I would still want to call it home, but I have moved on with my life. When I think about Jamaica, I remember the meandering of the Yallas River, the waters cascading off Dunn's River Falls, our endangered species of fern located at Fern Gully, the clear blue sea and beaches that rival any in the Caribbean. I reminisce on Bob Marley's "One love, One heart" and most of all a popular Jamaican song that united the country when we faced an economic crisis. It was a time when Jamaicans were leaving the island for the United States in search of a better life, "Sweet, Sweet Jamaica nah lef ya".

No other country in the world is quite like Jamaica and can be compared to life on the island. I love my home country as it has made me into the man I am today and yet I am so disgusted with its cultural values. Jamaica is one of the most culturally enriched islands in the world, yet it is a very poor country that depends heavily on tourism. Poverty at its worst looks like a crime. The few rich look down from their homes on the hills at the poor "savages" below. Behind the lush palm trees, the golden colors of the sun set at Rick's Café. Jamaica struggles with a staggering economy with high unemployment and social tensions and violence that is rooted in both the local and the international drug trade. The reality of my home is that when it is portrayed in the media, it is described as either a place to avoid or a great island destination. With all said and done, the island is considered one of the most homophobic societies on earth where men have been killed for even being thought of as homosexual or burnt alive for engaging in what is called ungodly sexual acts. Homophobia pervades the culture that the Government, despite its moral conscience refuses to lift the ban on homosexuality even in this global age of communication free liberties. There is a secret that no one wants to talk about and that is the reality that so many young men and boys are subject to incest and sexual abuse daily.

In a society that deems homosexuality an evil act punishable by imprisonment of up to ten years hard labor, it is hard to believe that there are a total of over fifteen reported cases each week of sexual abuse of young men and boys. One police rape unit reports that an estimated three cases are reported each week, and that is only one parish office. There are countless unreported cases from abused young men who are afraid of losing their lives. With all this argument and nonsense about Jamaicans being homophobic, who might I assume is responsible for all these rapes of our men and boys? We have kept silent for too long and our silence is deep rooted in history, our ancestors were raped as a means to keep them servile.

Jamaica is a strong nation; a nation filled with a history of fighters from Africa and that is where our story begins. We are descendants of the tribes of Ashanti, Yoruba, Ibibio and nations of the regions of Congo. The sad part of our history is that we as a nation have never accepted our history, as it was never truly told to us. We are a sexual people, filled with too much pride. I am not trying by any means to air my country's dirty laundry; I am merely stating facts and trying to entertain a meaningful conversation among Jamaicans and blacks in general. The outward appearance of slavery is over, and now we need to deal with the harsh reality of our society. We have kept our mouths shut for far too long. The burdens of slavery are still upon us and our men are crying, reaching out and needing to be heard. I feel deeply hurt that a man can take away the innocence of a child by one evil act and as a society, we blame the child, accusing the child of encouraging the act. The reality of it is locked behind that homophobic behavior which is an open aggression towards homosexuality. There is a lustfulness and deep-rooted willingness among men to experience the pleasures of another man. Is it wrong? I leave you the reader to make your own judgment. What is wrong is grown men preying on young kids. I will start the healing process; I AM A VICTIM OF RAPE AND I HAVE SURVIVED. The hardest part of recovery for me was coming out and admitting that I was sexually abused.

It is imperative that readers understand that sexual abuse is not about its victims; it is about what happened to them. Sexual abuse is a crime against you and not an indication of your sexual orientation. Sexual abuse has more to do with the violation of power, an act of aggression, control and manipulation. It is a crime against you the victim, as sex was used as a weapon, to control, dehumanize, humiliate and belittle you. Sexual abuse has nothing to do with lust, passion or love its all about the power dynamics. When a boy is sexually abused by a man, it is often incorrectly seen as a homosexual act. No single factor is more responsible for the stigma attached to male rape than homophobia, the irrational fear and hatred of homosexuality. Often at times, the majority of men who rape other men consider themselves to be heterosexual. As survivors, it is important to understand that, when you are forced, threatened or seduced into committing sexual acts, it does not mean you are a homosexual. Even if you enjoyed it or subjected yourself to abuse, the fact is that you were manipulated and your trust was violated. The harsh reality of abuse is that it steals your authentic self and identity and forces you to become shameful, confused, angry and hurt.

I have neither made attempts to justify or clarify homosexuality nor have I tried to condemn the act, as that was not my intention in writing this book. I have merely drawn a co-relation between incest and sexual abuse of men and the growing trend of homosexuality in Jamaica. I have attempted to analyze the cultural dynamics behind homosexuality and explain why a young boy at seven years old would kill himself after being raped by his school security guard. I share with you the reader an intimate side of me, the story of how I was molested at age four by my neighbor in the ghettos of Kingston, Jamaica. The book is more a reflection of my abuse and how I have survived and beaten the odds. I talk about trust and friendship and how my neighbor took advantage of that trust and raped me on a damp night at age fourteen and the reality of how this act of abuse transformed where we became lovers for two years. I am candid in both tone and language in my detailed account of the rape, and I give the reader the opportunity to be me for a moment as I give explicit details of the sexual act of rape. I talk about my struggles with alcohol through college, my obsession with killing myself and how I was able to balance school and achieve so much academically despite the odds.

I have dealt with the cultural dynamics of music and how it impacts on everyday life and how language, jargons, and slang helps to mold sexuality. There is an unedited chapter that deals with the general attitudes of current Jamaican social groups and how they view homosexuality. I have dished the dirt on the church, showing their hypocrisy in both thinking and teachings, as too many young boys while they kneel to pray after church service, are forced to ride the d———ks of their pastor who condemns the homosexual act each week in their sermons. Jamaica is a country filled with love and hatred and double standards that are deep rooted in slavery. I am attempting within the context of the church and their warped definition of sexuality to re-educate the black congregation about how sexuality was defined from a historical perspective and how European colonizers through slavery taught "US" blacks that sex was dirty. We have lived through centuries of the mis-education of the Negro race, and Christianity for centuries has been our opium and we need to put an end to it. I have researched the first use of the word homosexuality in the English version of the bible and discovered that there is no co-relation between sodomy, sodomite and homosexuality.

I have interchanged the chapters and tried to make the book more interesting to the reader. I have written the book with the innocence of a child. I had to relive my past, and become the naïve, vulnerable young boy I was who was somewhat clueless about the dangers of life. It is important that the readers bear this fact in mind, as in some parts of the book I am angry and I do not reason rationally and it is the built-up anger from my past talking. In reliving my past I became the young boy all over and it is he who is writing and not the adult me. I have dealt with the family and how it is important for parents to have a bond with their sons and stop defining masculinity based on penis size and the strength of a boy's voice. The family has an important role to play in helping to stop incest and sexual abuse of boys. Families need to face the reality that it can happen to their sons and by dismissing the issue like it never happen is creating an internal war within men that is causing a profound social ill. I have voiced the stories of boys who are trapped in a bar-less prison and who often remain speechless and I have given voice to their stories. I have also included the stories of mothers in pain, mothers who now regret blaming their sons for their abuse and who are now seeking forgiveness. I dealt with trust within the family and why it is important to listen to our kids.

Upon completion of the book, long before it was even published, I gave a talk to a group of men at a Sunday brunch in midtown Manhattan and at the end Wane a young man at the brunch, told me his story. Wane is twenty-one years old and currently resides in New York, and attends a prestigious law school in the city. After the meeting was finished, I saw this cute, sexy, confident young man with almond skin, bone white teeth and a smile that could brighten the world. He approached me. He thanked me for what I was doing and told me how brave I was to have taken up the burden of so many young Jamaican men. He was impressed that I was so candid in dealing with the rape and how much he admired the way I had asserted myself when I relayed my story. He wanted to know what inspired me to not commit suicide after all these years and I told him it was my belief in God and the strength of friendship. I believe we were all placed on earth for a profound reason and I think that I have now found my place. As he was about to walk away he looked me dead in the eyes as he held on to my hands and told me thanks again, he said in a soft voice, "I was raped by my mother's husband at age sixteen". At that moment, I felt his pain and tears came flowing down my cheeks. I knew then that all he wanted to do was talk and let it all out and I was happy that he felt confident to confide in me. I took Wane outside in the humid August night and comforted him allowing him to voice his innermost thoughts. Since I have written the book, so many men have told me their stories.

I found out that we had a lot in common, we grew up not far from each other in Jamaica, we went to the same church and I was two grades ahead of him in the same high school. He expressed his conviction in God and how much the church has been his support without the members knowing his pain and how he was suffering deep inside. It was on the day of the Lord, our sacred Sabbath that his stepfather raped him. He was sick that Sabbath morning and was unable to go to church; all his stepfather was doing in his mind was to check his temperature, but one touch led to another. At sixteen, he was six feet tall and weighed about a hundred and sixty five pounds, and was it not for the fact that he was sick he could have defended himself but he was too weak. His stepfather the man he had grown to trust and called daddy, ripped his pants off with force and strength and turned him face down on the bed and ripped him open with his ten inch thick hard muscle. It sounds cruel, yes it is, it happened and now we have to deal with it. His stepfather told him that if he told anyone, he would kill him and yes, he would as his gun was lying next to the bed to remind Wane that if he did talk, he would be dead. It happened three more times. It finally ended when he confided in his pastor at church who told his mother. His mother never believed him and it made him numb for years. His mother is still with the man and Wane no longer speaks to his mother. A family shattered. A mother-son relationship broken.

Throughout his entire story I closed my eyes and it was as if I were there, I felt his pain and anger. I gave him a hug and he wiped the tears from my eyes, I was angry most of all with his mother, as too many times mothers never believe. I must point something out, most young men who have been raped in Jamaica and who have fled and now call the US home, have beaten the odds and have excelled in school and soon enough will make a meaningful contribution to this country. Many have started and I give them all a "shout out", for being brave and for surviving. I ask these men to join me in an attempt to break the cycle; there is a young boy somewhere who is crying out, who needs to say stop. Let us be their voice. There is a chapter in the book that deals with healing and how to go about getting help as a victim of rape. I have listed a number of scenarios and if you answer yes to any of them, you have been sexually abused and you need to get help. Shutting yourself in a bar-less prison will do you no good; all it does is kill the soul.

I close the book with my last rape at age twenty-one and how I ran away from Jamaica. I blamed myself for the last rape as I felt I could have prevented it, it was not easy for me to accept that it was not my fault. Often times victims of sexual abuse think it is their fault but it really is not. You said no as a child, adults are there to protect you and they should never take advantage of that trust. I do not know why men are homosexuals, I do not know if it was a gift from God. I have even questioned if God is gay. I do not know all the answers, but I do know that there is a co-relation between being raped as a child and living the life of a homosexual. I close the book with forgiveness; the process of healing can never begin unless we first forgive ourselves. Oprah Winfrey has taught me one thing and that is true happiness comes from within, we must love ourselves first before we can love others. The queen of talk has given me hope and inspiration to share my story, and I thank her so much for her soul and the huge heart she has.

I hope that at the end of reading the book, you the reader will look at your husbands, brothers, uncles and sons differently. We are all men and we too have pain and at times are dying to let our burdens out. Slavery has ended but the aftermath of it still lingers. Society still uses a narrow ruler to define the masculinity of black men and it needs to stop, someone needs to break the cycle. I wrote this book for all the men and boys who are crying and yearning to speak out about their pains. I wrote this book because HIV and AIDS are both on the rise within black communities and women are being infected at an alarming rate. I write for my sister and my female cousins and aunts so that they may take the time to listen to their men and take the time to understand them and where they have been. As victims of abuse, we can never forget the abuse but we must first forgive ourselves and most importantly forgive our abusers, as they too need help. The memories will linger until death, but the healing starts from within.

***23 Child Sexual Abuse, Neglect, Maltreatment And Endangerment Allegations

© Jamaicans for Justice 2005
A Citizens Rights Action Group
Stella Maris Foundation Building,
1 Grants Pen Road, KINGSTON 8, JAMAICA, West Indies.
Tel:(876)755-4524-6—Fax: (876) 755-4355

Request for investigation as part of the official review of children's homes and places of safety ordered by Prime Minister, Rt. Hon. P.J. Patterson

***Allegations 1–4, children's names and alleged abusers names have been changed to protect their identities.

- Allegations 5–23, all names have been changed to protect identities.
- In each instance, allegation 1–23, individuals' and institutions' correct names have been provided to the review committee.

Sexual abuse, neglect and maltreatment of children at Reddie's home of safety and at Pringle children home, allegations

1. The alleged sexual abuse and neglect of a seven-year-old child, Michael Roberts, while Michael lived at Reddie's place of safety and at Pringle children's home. Michael lived at Reddie's since July 2, 1998 when he became a ward of the state, at age two and a half. MOH's Children Services Division transferred him to Pringle in May 2001, where he lived until I collected him on June 5, 2002, taking him to my home in the USA to adopt him. Michael accuses three workers of sexually assaulting him: Miss Bennett and Big Man at Pringle; Miss Roberts at Reddie's. These abuses are detailed in the attached document titled, **Michael Roberts: A Jamaican Child Severely Sexually Abused and Neglected While A Ward of the State.**

    1. The alleged sexual abuse of Winston, a child who is younger than Michael, who Michael says is similarly abused. The alleged sexual assault of Winston is described in the document titled, Michael Roberts: A

Jamaican Child Severely Sexually Abused and Neglected While A Ward of the State.

2. Five children of both genders—all under age seven when the alleged abuses occured — who lived at Reddie's and at Pringle while Michael lived in each home, who, it is alleged, frequently engage in sexual acts with each other, the boys frequently having sex with dogs at Pringle. The named children are Roy, Richard, Shirley, Marvin, Precious,

3. Two mentally retarded, disabled children, Bwoy Blue and Jim, who were frequent targets of sexual abuse by children living at Reddie's, it is alleged. Michael reports that, "plenty, plenty bwoy dweet wid 'im, 'im dumb, 'im can't talk, 'im is a idiot, 'im retard, 'im no know 'ow fe eat or 'ow fe play.... Bwoy Blue bite off one bwoy teely, it bleed bad bad bad bad....Me dweet wid Jim, 'im 'ave a big 'ead, it look funny....odda bwoy dweet wid 'im too, 'im no gat plenty sense...."

Sexual abuse, neglect and maltreatment of children who reside at various children's homes and places of safety, allegations

4. It is alleged that a 13-year-old boy, Lennox Cameron, complained that Molynes Chisholm Park Children's Home's House Father, Joseph Clarendon, sexually molested him. It is alleged that he reported the molestation in a letter he gave to a guidance counselor at Norman Manley High School. Allegations are that he wrote that the abuse occurred often and that he was going to kill himself. He reportedly said that Clarendon removed him from his bed at night and put him in Clarendon's bed where the abuse occurred. It is reported that Molynes Chisholm Park Children's Home management team, Rachel Morgan, Mother Sandra, Robert Lawson, Radella Murphy investigated the allegations then *"tried"* the case. During the investigation, two additional children, Radcliffe Long and Andrew Davis, allegedly accused Clarendon of sexually abusing them. During the "trial" Union Delegate, Mr. McKenzie, who attended the meeting, said the matter should be reported to the police, as it was a police matter. Reports are that Joseph Clarendon was found *"guilty."* No police report has been made. Joseph Clarendon was sent on paid leave then asked to resign. Reports are that Children's Services relocated the suicidal child, Lennox Cameron, to a different home. Lennox has not received therapeutic help.

5. Allegations are that Manville Square Children's Home's guidance counselor, Mr. Rodman Lawson, pulled Manville Square resident, Wendell Bloomington, out of school and kept him from attending school for a full week as punishment. It is alleged that Mr. Lawson further punished Wendell by requiring that he chop bushes with a cutlass from 8:00 a.m. to 4:00 p.m. each day for a week, working in the sun all day.

6. Allegations are that Manville Square Children's Home's guidance counselor, Mr. Rodman Lawson, punished two other male children, Lenmar Harper and Abner Nowden, in the same way. It is alleged that Lenmar and Abner were pulled out of school and kept from attending school for a full week as punishment. Allegations are that Mr. Lawson further punished Lenmar and Abner by requiring that they chop bushes with a cutlass from 8:00 a.m. to 4:00 p.m. each day for a week, working in the sun.

Informed sources say that while Lenmar chopped bushes on a Sunday, there was a heavy, *"all day rain."* It is alleged that Mr. Lawson forced Lenmar to *"continue chopping bush though the rain that was falling wet him up sopping wet,"* one informed source reports.

7. Orville Grandison lived at Sutton Parish children's home. He consistently returned home late from school. It is alleged that Zayman Cordell, Children Services children's officer responsible for Orville, would pick up Orville at school, and, contrary to regulations, take the child to his home before returning him to Sutton Parish children's home. This was reported to Mr. Cordell's supervisor who arranged a meeting to discuss the allegation. Reports are that the meeting was cut short when Mr. Cordell threatened a Sutton Parish worker in attendance. As a result, Children's Services Director, Mr. Bowen, informed the threatened worker that he, Mr. Bowen, would convene a meeting to further discuss the matter. The Sutton Parish worker has not heard from Mr. Bowen since then. The events occurred in 1998.

8. Odan Thompson lived at Sutton Parish children's home. He consistently returned home late from school. It is alleged that Zayman Cordell, Children Services children's officer responsible for Odan, would pick up the boy from school, and, contrary to regulations, take Odetta to his home before returning him to Sutton Parish This was reported to

Cordell's supervisor who arranged a meeting to discuss the allegation. The meeting was cut short when Mr. Cordell threatened a Sutton Parish worker in attendance. As a result, Children's Services Director, Mr. Bowen, informed the threatened worker that he, Mr. Bowen, would convene a meeting to further discuss the matter. The Sutton Parish worker has not heard from Mr. Bowen since then. The events occurred in 1998.

9. Young children at St. Mercy Children's Home often hear this goodnight lullaby at bedtime, *"All a uno go sleep, an' a don't want uno lickle batty-man sleep up nex' to one anadda."*

10. A man who frequents a children's home rapes a five-year-old resident. Years later, a male staff member at the home rapes the same girl. The home's management doesn't report either rape to the police. Both men are free to rape again. The raped girl receives no counseling.

Kay M. Osborne
Email: Kayosborne@aol.com

PART I
Sexual terms

I assume that you have decided to read this book either because you are curious about the subject, have been sexually abused at one point in your life or you have a friend or family member who has been sexually abused. In any case, you have made the right choice; sexual abuse affects everyone not only the victim. It is important to note that knowledge is power. Admitting to yourself or to others that you have been sexually abused is no easy task and most times men bury their emotions. The first thing you must do is to understand in your vulnerable state, you were manipulated. You were taken advantage of and the abuse was not your fault. The only way to heal is to first rid your self of the shame, guilt and denial of the abuse.

No two stories are the same and victims all react differently to sexual abuse. As an individual you are unique, but other victims do share many feelings in common, such as isolation, anger, low self-esteem, guilt just to name a few. Now this is where you break your silence. First on this book was difficult for me to write, it is no easy read. Now that the book is completed, I have learned so much about myself after breaking my silence and reliving the memories. I hope that by the end of the book you would realize that you are not alone and you may gather the courage to rediscover yourself. It will be difficult to open up at first but take baby steps, be confident or even confide in a trusted friend or seek professional help.

Here is your ticket to re-new your spirit and start the healing process. I implore you to read the recommended books at the end of this where you can get helpful incite into the healing process. Find a quiet place to sit and read all by yourself. Take a box of Kleenex and keep the phone next to you in case you may need to talk to someone. True happiness comes only from within. Now enjoy your journey release yourself and be free!

Sexual Abuse—Sexual abuse is all about power. It is when a person in power or authority forces you to perform sexual acts for him or her. Sexual abuse goes far beyond penal intrusion; it may range from the use of explicit pictures and language, to kissing and touching. It is a violation of your mind and body and it is sometimes used to keep you in a continued state of vulnerability.

Rape—Sexual assault or sexual violence perpetrated on a person by another against the will of the victim. Most rapes include force, intimidation, manipulation, cohesion or violence, acquiescence because of a verbal threat does not mean consent.

Statutory Rape—Sexual intercourse with an individual younger than the legal age of consent.

Gang Rape—Forcible sexual intercourse or other sexual activity committed on an individual by several persons.

Physical Sexual—Involving intercourse, oral sex, anal sex, masturbation of the child, having a child masturbate an adult, sexual touching (fondling), sexual kissing and sexual hugging.

Overt/Explicit—Involving voyeurism or exhibitionism.

Covert—Involving verbal sexual abuse or lack of appropriate boundary setting with the child.

Emotional Sexual—Involving enmeshment by the parent, child witness to sexual abuse or not providing appropriate and healthy sexual information.

Incest—Sexual relations between family members or close relatives, including children related by adoption. The act may include fondling, exposure, or penetration.

1

Confession

○ ○

In the beginning, God created the heaven and the earth. And the earth was without form and void: and darkness was upon the face of the deep. And the spirit of God moved upon the face of the water.

—*Genesis 1: 1-2.*

This was the long weekend I was waiting for it was mad fun. I met someone, he was already taken, but I didn't care about the person he was seeing! I was selfish, and I needed to be comforted and to feel loved. He was willing to offer both. The long weekend lasted for four days and I would do it all over again. We made hot, sweaty, passionate love and after sex, we lay in bed looking at each other. By the second day, he knew my birth sign, my mothers' middle name and what turned me on. The one thing that turned me on the most about him was that he listened and that is so hard to find in a lover. On the third day, we had brunch at Negril in the West Village, Manhattan and spent the rest of the day shopping in Macy's on Herald Square. On the last night, we held each other in our arms, hoping that it could last a bit it could last a bit longer but he had to return to his home in Jamaica and I had to continue with my lonely life. The morning he left my bed, I knew I was in love and it felt darn good and it was that love that inspired me to start this chapter. It has always been a dream of mine to write a book, but I never knew how to start. I wanted to be in love, to find a love of my own. Someone who loved me for me, someone who wanted to be with me and me alone, someone who wanted to take the time to know me for who I am, where I wanted to be and to dream with me. It sounds more like Karl Marx utopia. I know it can happen, I am still waiting for this dream to happen. I was inspired by this one guy who wrote an article in Essence Magazine, and he spoke about how, as he grew older he accepted himself more for who he is, the man that he has truly become.

Life is more like a journey and as we walk along the road of life, there are struggles that we must face. It is all about survival, and at times we feel as if we are in a world all by ourselves and that the troubles we face, we face them alone. This is far from the truth.

When I had finally decided to write the book, I had already given up my apartment in Brooklyn and I had walked off my job. (My supervisor was getting to me). I moved in with my best friend in Westchester and I commuted to Brooklyn each day to visit my friends just to relax my mind. On my way home from Brooklyn one night, I thought of where and how I started. In the beginning, God created the Heaven and the Earth. There are nights I go to bed, asking God if he really created me, if I was cursed or if he was punishing me for some long-time sin I committed as a child. I was told as a child that one should never question God but with all the pain that I have been through, I feel like questioning the devil himself. I have faith, I think, but I wondered what God thought about when he created me, in his own image. As you may have gathered, I am gay so is God one too? I have become somewhat comfortable in my "sin", but it was a journey that was long and filled with pain, rejection, denial, guilt, and most of all survival.

Of the memories of my childhood three of them stands out the most. I remember a "Hulk" lunch kit my mother had given me and she told me that it was a gift from my father and her. I was only four then, and like most Jamaican boys I have little or no memory of my father. The sad thing was that, this fat girl, named Antonette Brown, destroyed my lunch kit because she liked mine so much and could not get one. The lunch kit was replaced but it could never replace my "Hulk." Another memory occurred, one day in the blazing Jamaican sun late one afternoon; I had decided to climb the ladder at the back of the house, searching for some answer. I was only five. My neighbor who spent most of her days with my grandmother asked me what I was doing and I told her that I was walking to heaven, to ask God a question. I can still see Dora Lawson's face, laughing out loudly at what I had said. People said that God lived in the sky, so all I wanted to do was to go up as far as I could to talk to God, tell him about the feeling I had inside and was afraid to let out. By this time, I knew that homosexuality was wrong. It was a tabooed subject. At one point, I felt that only sick white men committed those acts of sexuality among themselves, and I was told that men who sleep with men would go to hell. All I wanted to do was to ask God why I always looked at boys and why I was fascinated with penises. This need for forgiveness led me to get baptized at age nine, thinking that the feeling would go away.

The third thing that stood out as a childhood memory has been haunting me for years and I still can not get it out of my mind. I was born in the countryside of Jamaica, not rural country but more suburban. My mother, being the rebellious woman that she still is, went to live in August-Town—a slum area of Kingston. She had a pretty decent job, and we lived in a tenement setting that my grandmother hated.

I remember when I was only five years old when my mother's neighbor's son, took me to a place that has changed my life up to this day. It was a hot day, the yard outside had no grass, the dirt was dry, and the humidity was high.

Mi no rememba him name, but him was tall, skinny and light skinned. Mi can see him face but it is a bit blurry. Him never did look cute, but him did looked like a fully-grown boy, him did sound like a man too. Everyone in the yard did use the same shower and I remember passing the shower on that hot summer day when him hold mi by the hand and teck me into the shower wid him. It was mi first time seeing a man naked and him did have hair all over him buddy, which fascinated mi most of all. Ah can still smell the scent of the orange carbolic soap that him did a use fi bath wid; him play with him buddy several times til it grow into a huge thing. It did start fi get thick, it was long, with lots of veins, and it seemed as if it was beating. It had the size of a tissue roll and it had a pink look wid a mushroom head. The soap was all over it and him did a rub him han up and down him long cocky slow. Ah was scared at first and mi did start fi shake, but mi remember looking down at mine, wondering why mine was so small and mi did want fi mi fi get long like him buddy. Ah remembered him holding mi hands to touch it and even though it did feel good, mi knew that something was wrong in what him was doing. As a child, mi was curious and it was that curiosity that forced mi to want to touch it.

Looking back at the memories all these years, I trusted him and looked up to him, his mother sewed for my mother and everyone looked up to this young man. It never occurred to me that someone I trusted would want to hurt me.

Mi lack me eyes them as him guide mi small and frail head to the tip of him buddy. Mi did a shake, mi could a feel the tears them a flow down mi face. Mi did want fi cry but most of all mi did want fi feel him buddy. Mi mouth was too small fi the head of him buddy but him did teck him time wid me, as him put it in and out of mi mouth.

This is the point where I am writing and crying at the same time. I am about to open a scar that has never been opened up in over nineteen years, it's hard but it's a journey I must start in order to stop these bad dreams. The tears are never ending, but in order to move on we must deal with our past and the inner demons we have, too many young boys have been through similar ordeals and we must break the cycle and speak out.

Ah can remember crying as him guide him buddy in and out of mi mouth, mi did try fi open mi mouth wider but ah could not, mi did a cry too much and the taste of it did meck me want fi vamit. Mi did want him fi stop, honestly, mi did really want him fi stop, but how mi did fi tell him fi stop, mi never did know. Him did older than mi and much stronga. What mi did a do did start fi hurt him as mi teeth was on it and mi did remember at one point mi bite down hard pan it. Although him never did lick mi, him teck it out and put it back in again. Fi tell you the truth, just looking at him face, the way how it did look pleasing as if mi did a do something good, did meck mi feel good inside mi self. But deep down widin ah myself mi did hate him, fi what him did a do to mi. Mi did more fraid a him when him start to put it in faster and faster, it did a meck mi jaw hurt, mi did try fi pull back mi head but him hold on tight tight to mi head. Me mouth did a hurt mi and it did full a spit and water did a drop from mi mouth like mi a dag. Mi could a feel him bady a shake and then him started to force it in futher in a mi moth, then mi feel something in a mi moth. Him never did want fi stop, it did feel like say him did a choke mi, then him pulled it out. It did too late fi mi spit and it go all the way down mi throat. When mi finally get a chance and pull back mi head all mi see was something white and thick, it did all over pan mi lip and mi mouth and it never did taste good. Mi later found out during puberty that the white milky-looking thing was sperm and it did use fi meck baby. All of a sudden him mood change and him push mi out of the shower.

I wanted to talk to someone but there was no one! I wanted to vomit but it could never come up, I lived with that taste in my mouth for years on end. He never threatened me, and I knew I could not tell anyone. I was afraid that if I spoke out, I would be beaten. I felt as though this was my fault and I never wanted anyone to know what I had done. Later that evening he saw me, and he just walked pass as if nothing happened, I smiled at him and he looked at me with anger in his eyes. More was to come my way that night to change me up to this day.

When the moon is full in the tropics, it makes you think that you are at peace with God and his creation. That night the moon was full. I remembered being one of the children in the yard singing, "moonshine baby" we gathered rocks and placed them around each other. It was an African ritual I believe (I am yet to know the significance of the stones and the moon). My memory was vivid. It was later that night and he was coming from somewhere fancy, as he was all dressed up. He went to the back of the yard, and I followed to see where he was going. He was hiding in the dark and as I passed by him, he grabbed me and held me in a firm grip. He pulled me closer to him and reminded me not to tell anyone of what had happened earlier that day. I was only a child and in a misguided way I felt loved by this man, my head reached his crotch, and I felt the hardness of his manhood, the thing that was once small had become huge.

Him teck out him buddy and this time him never put it in a mi mouth, all him do was to rub it pan mi face. Where mi and him was, was dark and mi could a see the moon reflection pan him. Him pull mi down to the cold concrete floor and put him buddy next to mi back. I had not one clue what him was about to do to mi, all mi can remember is that him did start fi pull down mi shorts, and him touched mi in that one spot that no man should. Oddly enough, later in life I found out that, that one spot could have given me more pleasure than I could have ever imagine. Him never put it in but him did try fi put it in. Every time him try fi put it in it did hurt me but mi was curious to know what him did ago do from behind mi. At that age, mi mind was not that fully develop and mi could not have imagine what could have happened.

I felt vulnerable, I felt compelled to do as he said. I honestly had no clue what he was doing or what could have happed, but it felt good, the touch, the feel, and the look on his face.

It was not long before my absence from the group was felt and I heard my grandmother calling out for me. I heard her footsteps approaching us in the dark. We were both scared. We were cold, but all grandma did was held me forcefully by the hand and led me away. She knew something occurred and she said nothing to me, she looked me dead in the eyes and she said nothing. It was our secret and she died without us ever talking about it. I hated her for doing that to me, but I have forgiven her now. What was she to do, in the fabric of the Jamaican society, homosexuality was a sin, and a man could be killed if he was suspected of such an act. Homosexuality was condemned in all forms of cultural lifestyle. The music spoke out about it and the language and jargons spoke of it. "Batty man fi dead" "All who no like batty man hole up yu hand" "We ago kill a boy if we catch him a fuck batty." At a tender age I knew I was a homosexual, those two acts alone confirmed it to me. Its so messed up, but Jamaicans are so much against the act of homosexuality, even if a child or an adult were molested or raped, they too were seen as being a homosexual and would be condemned for life.

My Grandmothers' stern look and silence strongly suggested that I was at fault and I had pushed myself upon this young man. I lived with that guilt for years and now it is my time to let go of the guilt and move on. I was only a child and I was abused. I would love to sit down and tell grandma that I never did and that I understood why she said nothing to me. At times, I wondered had she said something to me, if my life would have turned out differently, but only God in his Heaven knows that it happened for a reason. My grandmother's silence on the incident went on for years. We never spoke about it. I had the greatest of love for her, she knew something was wrong and she always protected me. She was my world, and anytime I was angry only she alone could comfort me. She was light skinned, half-white, and with long "jet black" hair. She had the smile of an angel, wide, with perfect white teeth. She had a mole under her left eye and each time I was close to her, I would touch it. She was medium built, and she walked assuredly with grace. There are days when I sit by myself and I can hear her voice, she used to call me Rassy, and the softness of her voice in my head would calm me down. Whenever I get angry and feeling all alone, I would close my eyes and listen to her voice and it would put me at peace with myself.

I was once embarrassed to talk so openly about my childhood past. I was most of all ashamed for enjoying what the guy did to me and most of all that I wanted him to do it to me again. As the years went by, I thought less about what happened as I was now back in the country and living a healthy childhood. I knew that I was different; I acted different and sounded different too. I was more feminine than most of the boys at school and they jeered me a lot. I had a very supportive family and most of my attention was placed in my schoolwork. I knew I was different so I had to excel in something other than sports, which most times I was not allowed to play with my peers. School was all I had, and I just wanted to read and get the grades. I knew I had committed a sin against God, and it was my deepest dream to become a pastor when I got older, then I knew God would forgive me for my sins.

I was the first to go through puberty in my small group of eight, and my friends were all fascinated by new discoveries. I used to take showers outside on weekends but I now saw pubic hair and felt that I was becoming a man and now had to take showers indoors. I recall one morning at the age of ten, when my neighbor's granddaughter came over the house. She used to come by early in the mornings when my mother left for work and on this particular morning I was a man and I saw the signs of it. It was common for us to play with each other, I enjoyed putting my index finger between her legs, it never had a pleasant scent but she enjoyed the feel and I felt good knowing that she liked what I did. I was now a "girls' man", and my penis was growing, much to the size of the guy in my past.

It was late December and it was windy outside. She came over the moment my mother left for work and she took off all her clothes. Though she was much younger than I, the fact that I was with a girl made all the difference.

I was wearing a red alligator-print brief and it was my favorite one. We were on the floor of my mother's living room, and similar to what I had seen on a porn tape, I was to put my fingers as I always do and then put my penis inside of her. I did as I saw on the TV and it felt f___king great, she was crying but she never asked me to stop and I never wanted to stop either. I became Christopher Columbus that morning when I felt a tingling feeling in my back and it hurt but felt good at the same time. My underwear was on through all of this, I pulled my penis out and I saw the same white milky thing that came from that guy in my past all over my brief. I ran to the shower and scrubbed my skin over ten times while the girl lay in pain on the floor. I hated her, I wanted to hit her and I screamed at her to leave and never come back. I hid the underwear in my dresser drawer and it was there until I was 20 years old. I not only discovered sperm and what my body was capable of producing but I also discovered the art of masturbation. I hated when the milky thing came from my penis, but I enjoyed the feeling most of all.

This new-found hobby was masturbation, which I did every day, sometimes three times per day. One day I was home alone and I did it so much, I saw nothing came from my penis and I was scared. The odd thing about all this was that I had no brother or father figure to talk to about this entire new discovery; with his absence I taught myself how to be a man by reading books. I haven't quite outgrown that newfound hobby and it is still my hobby now I'm 24 years old and it will continue for a long time. I still do it almost every day. I was a skilled masturbator and I was happy I was never caught. I yearned, most of all for a brother, someone to whom I could tell all that was going on. The boys in the neighborhood still did not accept me, even when I tried to reach out to them. My best friends were my books. The one real friend I had, we used to masturbate together. We were the same age; my mother and his mother were very good friend and we were a few days apart at birth. I enjoyed going over to his house to play. I felt all we had in common was putting our penises together and stroking it. It was not until later on in my adolescent life that this boy changed the course of my life and opened my eyes to the forbidden world. A world I promised myself never to re-enter; but it was not meant to be.

Now at twenty-four I don't have many pleasant memories of my childhood. It is sad that the few experiences I can recall were those I mentioned previously in this chapter. I strongly believed that I was tremendously affected when I was sexually abused as a child and it has erased most of my pleasant memories, as I should have had some. David Finkelhor, *Early and Log-Term Effect of Child Sexual Abuse: an Update* gives a compelling study on the impact of sexual abuse on children. In a joint research with Angela Browne (Brown & Finkelhor, 1986) they mentioned that the most common symptoms relating to child sexual abuse are fear, anxiety, depression, anger, aggression and sexually inappropriate behavior. In regards to its long-term effect, they argued that the most frequently noted patterns include depression, self-destruction, and anxiety, feeling of isolation and stigma, poor self-esteem, difficulty trusting others, a tendency towards seeking legitimization, substance abuse and sexual maladjustment.

I can clearly relate to most if not all of the short and long-term symptoms listed by the study. While I have learnt to deal with the abuse, I am still filled with anger, not towards my abusers or myself but more towards my family, who have yet to accept the reality of my abuse. I have a huge difficulty trusting others and I still feel isolated from my surroundings.

Brown & Finkelhor, in their study argued that, most of the new research conducted on the early and long-term effects of Childhood sexual abuse has simply reinforced and consolidated what their earlier research found. They further pointed out that their 1986 article no longer conveyed the flavor, scope and energy as larger, more detailed and more sophisticated studies are now available. The new studies currently available consist of additional efforts to establish a correlation between the history of sexual abuse and a variety of mental health symptoms and pathologies to demonstrate that sexual abuse does have a noxious impact both initially and in the long term.

The Impact of Abuse on Boys

The majority of literatures I have read on the impact of sexual abuse on boys have suggested that there is a comparative gap between boys and girls. While I have no certification in the field of psychology, I have interviewed and come in contact with over 350 men and in my opinion they have found it much harder to cope with sexual abuse than the few women I knew who were sexually abused as children. I might add that the sample of young men was taken from within the social context of the Jamaican society

Brown and Finkelhor, in their article pointed out, that they found few surprises in their research. The article states that boys, like girls, show a marked impact as a result of sexual abuse both early and long term. The study shows that the response of boys might have been expected to be more different for several reasons. It is accepted that victims of sexual abuse including the violence of rape—both boys and girls, do suffer from issues relating to their sexual identity. In spite of this, Brown & Finkelhor concluded that in the available research on boys, there are far more similarities that differences.

Sexual abuse of both boys and girls is not confined to the home. They extend to situations outside of the home. In most of the young men I spoke to who were sexually abused, there were no father or male figure within the home and they were abused by a close family friend or someone of authority outside of the home. Finkelhor research further notes that, when there are other differences between boys and girls, the ones most often noted are along the dimensions called *"internalizing"* and *"externalizing"* (Friedrich, Urquiza & Beilke; 1986 Friedrich, Beilke, & Urquiza, 1987,1988). Boys are more often reported to be acting aggressively, such as fighting with siblings (Gomes-Schwartz, Horowitz, & Cardarelli, 1990; Tufts, 1884), and girls are more often reported to be acting depressed. More in-depth analogy of the impact of sexual abuse on boys can be found in chapter 17. Throughout this book, evidence of how sexual abuse has impacted my life is evident. The intimate journal entries through the book will give a true reflection of my emotional state.

2

Ne Me Quite Pas

○ ○

"Jut because you've loved and lost don't stop loving. It's so necessary as a human to love and feel it, to hurt and to acknowledge it. Because that's where you get these amazing lessons from. It's okay to hurt, even if you're the one that's getting played, that's how you learn".

—Jill Scott

It took me over a week to start Chapter 2, but God must have had a profound reason to not allow me to go sit around that computer. "I put a spell on you"—Nina Simone was playing in my head all week long and I had to change the focus of the book. May 2004 issue of Essence had an article on Sexual Abuse: Tackling a Taboo, based on the novel *No Secrets No Lies: How Black Families Can Heal from Sexual Abuse*, by Robin D. Stone. Stone wrote about her own experience with sexual abuse and did extensive research on the subject. It gives a compelling collection of stories and survival strategies in her book. It is a moving book as it speaks to black families, asking them to fess up with the reality that sexual abuse does exist in our families and that our men and boys are afraid to talk about it because of the stigma society has placed on the subject. There is no time but the present for blacks within the African Diaspora to deal with our cultural and social ills. HIV and AIDS are on the rise and it's killing our women. One reason for this is that far too many men within the black community refuse to acknowledge their homosexuality. As a result, we have to face the harsh reality of the consequences of men who refuse to admit that they are gay or bisexual. Our men, brothers, fathers, sons and husbands are hurting and they need to get over the pain and anger they are going through, but as a people we must be able to open up to them and accept the truth. It's a problem that as a collective group we can solve.

Colonialism has had a profound impact on the lives of many blacks. Slavery has ended. Segregation has ended yet we still feel the heavy arm of racism and we still define masculinity by the same fabric of power that once held us in bondage. Too many young men like myself have been scared to come out and deal with the truth, as we know for a fact that our families would not be accepting of the reality of the abuse. We say as a people we want to move on, but in order to strive for the future, we must sit as a family and deal with our dark secrets and lies that we carry for generations to generations. Our women, our mothers, sisters and wives have a responsibility to listen and give us the opportunity to be open. Mothers need to teach their sons how to be emotional, to cry and to say how they feel; it's the only way to break this cycle. To be a man is more than being tough, rough and providing for the family. Just as how girls are taught to be emotional and express themselves, so too should our boys. Dealing with abuse and sexuality among us as a race, we are dealing with our past and protecting our children and our grandchildren.

The more I gather information about sexual abuse and incest, I no longer feel trapped in my bar-less prison, and in which I was forced to live my life for so many years. I still question my masculinity and now accepting my sexuality does not make life any better. Too many times I have to "shake it off" and keep silent even when I was in pain or even angry. Whenever I have a headache, I don't take pills; all I do is sleep it off. To me taking pills would make me dependent on something else other than me and I feel it would make me less of a man. The reality of all this is that after the sleep the problems are still there. I have treated my problems like a nightmare, hoping that when I wake up, it will be all over. I still do have problems sleeping, my solution is masturbation, and however I never ejaculate. By the time I reach my sexual peak, it takes a lot of energy to hold it back, it leaves me weak and restless and I eventually fall asleep like a baby.

It was never easy growing up, I was the only male in the house other than my uncle and most of my ideals of manhood were what I heard from my mother and her female friends. I was expected to act like a man, I was silently taught to be, strong, brave, resourceful, independent and most of all in control. I defied the odds and at times I did show signs of emotions and yes, the boys in the neighborhood considered me a punk and a sissy. It's a sad thing that young black boys' fear showing emotion because of how they were socialized.

I was raised in the "old school" and being with a man was a sin, the greatest sin of all. I used to feel guilty, isolated, depressed as I felt that I had allowed the abuse to happen. Often at times, I ask myself why I never fought him off and why I refused to say anything about it to someone. It felt at times that I found pleasure in what he did. I was forced while growing up to live by society's expectations and I had concerns about my masculinity and more importantly about my sexuality. One of my greatest fears of being silent all these years was the fear of being tagged a homosexual. I felt that the act alone would make me gay and I thought that the act would draw me closer to being gay and even want to indulge more in the sexual act. I remembered the night when I revealed to my mother that I was sexually molested and her reaction to what I had told her. She openly questioned if I enjoyed it. I was confused for years, fighting with questions for which I had no answers to; I was terrified of coming "out', so I had to hide. The severe homophobia I grew up around made life a living hell, it also forced me to become a man before my time but in the end, I have survived.

April 9, 2004, 8:10 PM,

I woke up to the ringing of my phone, when I picked up, all I heard was the sound of crying from my youngest friend asking me what he should do? At first, his words were unclear, but I was no longer sleepy and I was fully awake to listen to him. It was obvious from his sobbing that he was in pain hurting from something, and I was willing to comfort him. He told his mother, a Jamaican mother that he is gay. He never wanted to, but she was nagging him too much about his friends, where he was going and with whom. She was petrified and wasn't supportive of the fact that he is gay and that it hurts knowing that he is. She wasn't mild on words. She cursed him in the name of the Lord. Eternal damnation was now on him and he felt the world was on top of him and he never wanted to be alone. I am but only twenty-four years old, and too many times have I listened to myself and many other young black men cry, trying to fit into the world that our parents have brought us. It's not easy to deal with the pain of even admitting to ourselves that we are gay and its even more traumatizing to open up to our families.

Often times I have prayed to God, asking him to take my life away while I sleep as the pain that I have been through no man my age should have to go through. Being a homosexual in the black community is living in hell, and if most of us could live our lives over we would not live this life and we would ask no one to live it either. I have dreamt of a pill or a liquid that could cure me. I had felt at one point in my life that I was sick. I had a disease that could be cured but the reality of the matter is that I am not sick. I have dreams and aspirations like any other young black male. Yes, I have beaten the odds of the life expectancy of most black men and I have excelled academically at an early age.

Oddly enough, I felt that only men could rape or molest boys, but to my surprise women do it too. I had just moved to New York and I met this cute Jamaican guy on Christopher Street. He came up to me talking about God and how God has changed his life but honestly; I was convinced that he was using God to make a pass at me. I never attended church with him that weekend but we decided to hang out some more each week. The friendship evolved into something more real when he told me that he was Jamaican and he no longer had the accent as he came here when he was fourteen. He was thirty-one when we met.

He came to my house one weekend and I was going to cook a Jamaican meal for him and watch some TV. I love to cook so it was fun to have him over and it was my first apartment so I was excited. The evening was going great and there was a program about rape on the TV and as always each time I saw anything about children being raped I would get upset. He saw the passion in my eyes and immediately we started a conversation about rape and incest. I told him that I was molested and raped and he was a bit sad and he gave me a hug and told me how sorry he was that it happened to me. I became teary eyed and he prayed with me for about a minute and told me that God had a plan for me and that one-day my story will change a life and help break the cycle.

The conversation took a twist when he told me that a neighbor also molested him. He was the first adult to ever confess to me that he was molested and it gave me so much comfort only God in Heaven could explain how I felt that day. He didn't give me much detail about what happened but it was obvious that he was still feeling the hurt. I asked him at one point during the conversation if he still keep in contact with the person or if he ever told his family about what had happened and then he gave me the shock of my life. The person who molested him was not a man it was a woman. Out of ignorance, I started to laugh at him. I knew he felt hurt and now, writing about it, I felt sorry for what I did, but I was naïve to the fact that women did such cruel acts. To an extent, I felt that a woman doing such a thing to a young boy should never be considered as rape. I felt it was the natural thing to do, he was a boy she was a woman; she was just showing him what it was like to be a man. It was right in my eyes. I knew many boys during their teenage days that would be happy to have a woman touch them in a sexual manner.

Separate and a part from the hurt that he still feels about what had occurred in his past, he has not dealt with the issue and it has caused him a lot of failed relationships with women. He has never committed a homosexual act but on several occasions he said that he feels more comfortable being around men but based on his upbringing from home, he found it hard to be with a man sexually. As most men do, they try based on social norms and sanctions, to suppress these desires for men. Up to the age of 31years, he has never had a successful relationship with a woman, they all failed, as there is a part of him that needs to open up and it is obvious to these women that he has something to hide. Even though he loves to be with women and he wants to have a successful relationship with one, he has a certain level of distrust for women, which makes his relationships difficult. In addition, he gets a bit withdrawn during sex and he has become physically abusive during sex on several occasions.

With all this pain and anger from his past, it will take forever for him to heal. Sadly enough based on how we were socialized, some women will see him as being weak if he makes a big issue out of such an incident. What will it take for us to realize that our boys and men are hurting? The moment a man gets close to his emotions he is put down or considered weak. No wonder gay men have so many choices as so many of them are willing to do what women over the years have refused to do, listen and not judge. I later found out that my friend was not the only one who has been molested by a woman and often these young men never consider it to be rape. In my mind if its two young boys experimenting or a boy and girl, sure that is cool, as that is childhood innocence but to have an adult, someone who should protect you, force themselves on you as a child that is wrong. Even if the child likes it and wants it to happen, again it is still wrong. As Oprah once said, "it is the adult's responsibility to protect the child. It is wrong for an adult to seduce a young child—to engage in a sexual act."

This is my journey through survival. I have read and listened to many stories of boys, who have been through depression, who have kept the anger of abuse locked up inside them for years. At one stage in my life, I felt it was wrong to cry as it was a sign of weakness but as a grown man, I realized that crying was a sign of strength. It was the crying that kept me focused on my books, as I knew God had a plan for me. Yes, I had given up on prayer but I had to survive, not for me but for my children, so that they would never go though what I have had to live with. Depression is not easy for any man; it leads him to do so many things, things that go against what he was taught at home. We ask ourselves why so many men are in prison and why is it so many men are angry, but have we ever asked them why? All it takes is a listening ear, someone who would give you the time of day to listen to the pain you are going through and tell you that it's going to be all right and that someone cares. As the book unfolds, you will see my pain, feel my hurt and anger, and jump the hurdles I had to jump, it wasn't easy but I am glad to say that I am alive to tell the tale.

I say to all young men out there even those who are much older, who have at some point in their lives been molested or raped to take the time to reflect on the past. No matter how much we try to hide the fact that we have been molested; it will live with us until we talk about it. It is okay to cry, its natural, and its much better to cry than to channel the anger in a negative direction. So far based on my research, most men who commit acts of rape have been raped or molested themselves before. It is a sad story when a man has to commit an act such as this, especially seeing that it also happened to him. Oddly enough, it's all about power and these men use what society teaches them as power to regain control over their lives. Sexual abuse is a form of power struggle when someone uses sex to dominate another. It is not so much the act itself that is used as the power but rather the tool that is used to create the act, the penis. A man sees his penis as his ultimate strength, the bigger his penis the more strength he has. When a man rapes a young boy or a man, it's all about showing dominance and who is in control. From my reading I have noticed that, men are raped during war by their captors to weaken them and to dehumanize them.

I have been doing research on the impact of sexual abuse on young boys and men and how it has affected them for over three years. Sometimes young boys grow up to molest younger men, because the forced sexual act of rape lingers within them and it makes them weak as men. To regain their masculinity they unintentionally go out and seduce young boys and the cycle starts all over. As I have done throughout the book, I put myself in the places of these young men and try to figure out why they would want to do this to someone. It all narrows down to pay back time, revenge, an attempt to heal, an attempt to gain attention from the outside world that they need help. Men find it more difficult to express them selves and sometimes, I myself do lean on younger men for emotional support. Some where within them, that child that was abused is trapped and needs to be let out, to free himself from all the pain that he is going through. By bonding with younger men, some men find it easier to deal with that past, most times, they get so emotionally attached to these young men, they believe that the only way to show affection is through sex. It isn't for society to blame them or even denounce them as men. They were taught that their emotions could not be shown outside of the context of sexual intercourse. Most young men who are sexually molested were abused by a close family member or a close family friend whom they trusted and loved. They interpreted this love in the same context as the bond they have developed with younger men. They believed that their abusers loved them and so they seduce younger boys in an attempt to show them love and affection by having sex with them.

**Brandon 46, Jamaican
Resides in Brooklyn, New York**

"I once raped this fourteen year old boy who lived in Bedford Stuyveson in Brooklyn when I was in my mid thirties. I used to be his mentor in a Church program for boys who were fatherless. I was driven to him as he reminded me of me when I was his age, he was witty, full of life and energy and he loved playing chess. I don't know but I felt so close to him, each time we met I just wanted to hug him, to hold him, nurture him and give him the love I never got. I knew he liked me as he spoke about me to everyone he knew. I seduced him, and I am sorry, (crying) it hurts, I saw myself that night when I pinned him down on the bed and forced myself on him. That was the last night I ever saw him, I wanted then, and still do want to apologize to him but how do I? I made an honest mistake and I live with that guilt everyday."

I am not trying by any means to justify the actions of these men as it is wrong, unacceptable and they should be punished. I do not only see them as abusers but as victims themselves, who need help as much as these young men who they have seduced. Brandon was raped by his stepfather, while he lived in Jamaica. He loved his stepfather and even called him daddy; he saw the abuse as love a sign of affection. Even though he felt that it was wrong, he believed that if he had talked about the abuse, maybe he would understand why he went back for more or why he felt so emotionally attached to his stepfather. My self and many others, who have been abused, can relate to Brandon and the affection he had towards his abusers and why he never spoke up. While the actions of abusers are wrong, they too need help. There is a greater meaning behind their actions. For some men who have never been abused and commit sexual acts of violence against young boys, it is all about power and control.

What is needed is open dialogue with our young boys. Sexual abuse of young boys and men is not new to Jamaica or within black communities. There is a simple solution to the problem, talking and more talking. We as a group need to go beyond cultural denial and fear. We need to explain to our boys what love is and then extend that to defining what touch is acceptable and what is not acceptable. We need to encourage the victims of sexual abuse to get help and not see them as having a problem or to let them feel that it was their fault. It is our responsibility to help those men who have abused young men, as they too may be victims. The definition of sex needs to change and we need to move away from the notion that sex is only for procreation and not for pleasure. If we condemn our boys and men from a simple act of masturbation, which is natural we force them to release these sexual tension elsewhere. Encourage our men and boys to know themselves touch their penises, and teach them that nothing is wrong with self-pleasure. It is the sex. I have never seen hair grow in the palm of my hands because of masturbation nor have I gone blind. Some of the more popular myths. Sex is not love and love is not sex. Sex enhances love when done in an emotional context as it brings two consenting individuals closer together. Give boys the freedom to be open to express themselves so that when they have been touched incorrectly they can speak out.

3

Love Wouldn't Count Me Out

○ ○
"By the time I entered Morehouse College, I saw being gay as something normal and I treated it as such."

—*Larry L. Walker*

Manhood came on me quite fast, by the time I was ten years old, I had fully matured into a young man. My voice had changed; my body all over had developed. I entered high school, at age ten, one of the youngest in my class, but I feared high school, feared being called a faggot and I feared dealing with my peers, thinking that soon they would know my secrets. My older sister and I attended the same high school, and although it gave me a sense of security, it still was not enough to comfort me. The reality of it all was that she could not protect me from what I was to discover in high school, she did play a role later on in my life in terms of healing and for that, I am grateful.

Throughout high school, I refrained from participating in sports. I knew I had a liking for boys and never felt comfortable hanging around them during any form of physical activity. I was now having frequent erections, and being around boys would trigger one off. It would make my attention to them too obvious. My pubescent years were not much help, as it made me more and more confused about who I was. I fought with myself to deal with how I was feeling and it made me become more outspoken, assertive and abrasive. I developed a passion for reading. Though it never showed itself in my grades. I was okay with that, as it was my way of not drawing attention to myself. I never like much attention, for I feared my secret would be revealed. I was never popular in school, yet I was well liked. Everyone knew that O'Brien stood up for what he believed in and I never gave a f__k. about what people thought of me.

It was my second year in high school and I was to once again discover the pleasure of sex during physical education in the shower room at school. As always, I would hide from my physical education teacher as I dreaded going to class, so I hid myself in the shower room one day. My childhood playmate that also attended the school and was in my class came in to urinate and his penis was visibly hard. He came over to me and out of curiosity, I touched it, but to my surprise, he did more than touch mine, he put his lips on them, the same way the young man from my past forced me to do to him. That day I discovered oral sex, and oh my God! It felt darn good, and now I knew why the guy from my past wanted me to do it to him so badly.

Ah had on mi gym shorts and him just move mi shorts up a bit more and him started playing with the head of mi cocky. The feeling it did a give mi did a kill mi. Mi did want fi scream out the way how it did feel good. Just the way how Devon did meck up him face, like say him love it too much, meck mi did want fi do it to him. But mi couldn't.

School was still in session, the fear of being caught, even worst killed was in my mind but this new discovery was too much and I never wanted it to stop.

Him never did do it ruff, him did a just move it in a out a him mouth. Mi did cum so quick and to ma surprise him teck it all in. Him never say a word to me after that. Him just get up wipe him mouth and walk outside. Mi did want fi go outside but mi did fraid the bwoy them outside would see me and see the look of guilt pan mi face.

I was now more convinced that I was a homosexual and I sought refuge in the church, like most black men. The Bible was my shield and the word of God was my sword. The church was my hiding place and the world was my enemy. There was never a week that I would not cry in church. I had already been baptized and a full Christian serving the Lord and I felt guilty in the eyes of the Lord. Being in church never helped much, what it did was to escalate my problems. There were Sabbaths when pastor would preach about homosexuals and that they would go to hell and that God destroyed Sodom and Gomorrah for that reason. The topic of homosexuality was not treated with much justice. It's ironic that the place where we seek love and affection the most, was the same institutions that hate and rebuked homosexuals as if they too should not be loved. The church took the laws of God and turned love into hate. It was difficult finding someone to talk to, so all I did was pray, and ask God for eternal salvation and begged for his forgiveness. I have contemplated suicide many times and tried but each time I would fail. I could never cut myself I hated the sight of blood and the knots in the ropes would never hold.

My newfound love of oral sex brought me further away from God and it did not bring me any closer to Devon. Devon gave me a chance to express my sexual side. We never spoke about it, it was an understanding that we would meet up before school or after school and he would give me oral sex. There were times when he had asked me to return the favor and I refused he said he would never do it again. For fear of losing such pleasure, I did it. I hated how it felt and most importantly, it brought back painful memories. I could never do it for long for I never had much interest, and I did it only because I wanted him to do what he did best. I never swallowed his semen. It tasted bad and I felt that I would get sick if I ever did. By the time I was twelve years old I had mastered the art of oral sex.

On several occasions, Devon told me that it was going to be the last time we were going to do what we were doing. No matter how hard we tried, we could not stop. I am not saying that I was innocent in this but he used to beg me to allow him to have oral sex with me, and being a friend I obliged. Over the years, I have tried to analyze Devon and why we were never close as friends and why we only had one thing in common with each other, sex. At a point, it went far beyond childhood innocence, as we were both conscious of what we were doing. Looking back on Devon now and the way he reacted towards me and the things he did, it's quite obvious that he was dealing with his own issues. Devon's mother was more open and relaxed compared to my mother and he drank on a regular basis and often times would get drunk. He started smoking marijuana from an early age and he hung around older men.

I have grown to see some of the men he used to hang around with and it is a known fact that they are homosexuals. They live on the down low and I wonder to myself if at any point Devon was molested by any of these men. His knowledge of gay sex had to come from somewhere. Jamaican society is not that open and back then, there was no "Queer as Folks", or "Six Feet Under" so someone had to put some of these thoughts into his mind. Whenever he approached me, he seemed well verse as if he had done it with someone before and he often claimed that he never did.

Childhood sexual experiment can also lead to sexual abuse. I used to live in the countryside of Jamaica, which was synonymous for its flat terrain, and numerous rivers. Often times I would joke with my friends about river sex but it is real, many boys get raped during childhood sexual experiment at rivers. When I was much younger, it was common to see young boys taking baths naked at the river. It was often a group of boys who were seen swinging from a tree branch or a vine into the river. Often at times, there was an older boy who was a part of the group who was going through puberty. During puberty, an erection was as common as taking a leak. Out of curiosity the younger boys may want to touch the older one's penis and it is encouraged as it is seen as just child's' play, but it can get out of hand.

There was an incident with two cousins who went to the Cabarita River in Westmoreland and the older boy attempted to force his erect penis on the younger boy. While the younger boy was not penetrated, it is still sexual abuse and up to this day, my friend talks about it. He does not see it as abuse but it is. There are so many other stories similar to the one noted above as it is done all in the name of child's play. There is also an incident where a teenaged girl about sixteen forced herself on an eleven-year-old boy. As a child, I have heard many such stories but now I know that it is rape, and not child's play. It may be seen as a right of passage in the eyes of some individuals but it may have psychological problems later in the young man's life. He may find it difficult to engage in sex, have sexual dysfunction, or more often pre-mature ejaculation. Even oral sex is seen as an inappropriate sexual practice.

I never had a dislike for girls, I had many wet dreams thinking about them but I realized from early that if I saw a boy and a girl I was more prone to giving the boy more attention. I had two very close girlfriends in high school and to this day they are still in my life, thank God for them as they have loved me unconditionally. Natasha and Jeannine were all I had, I developed friendship with others but these two girls had my back no matter what. They have grown to become educated women who are in search of a man but it is so difficult for them to find one. These are women who would listen to men and even though their men were abused, they would still see them as men and they would give them the love and comfort that was needed to heal and try and live a normal life.

There were nights in high school when I would pray to God asking him to give me the courage to talk to a girl. There were a few I liked and would love to talk to but I was shy. Me shy, it's hard to believe but I am shy somewhat. I was not afraid of girls but more afraid of rejection and the fear of them knowing what I had been through and I could not deal with that. I was also scared of being in the company of boys as young boys can be vindictive at times and allow you to loose your self-esteem if you don't act like them or try to be a fool by trying to sleep with every girl in school.

I never had many friends and still don't have a lot. I now have a select group of five men that are more than friends. They are more like family as they stood beside me when my family turned their backs. I never liked the company of boys as I found them to be rather repulsive and they think about the wrong things, sex and girls. Church and school were my life and God was and still is my best friend, as only He knew how I felt and what I have been through. I lost God's friendship at one point, but I am back in his company and only he alone can forgive.

My adolescent years were filled with more and more confusion and denial of what myself and Devon were doing. I got low grades in school and most of my free time was spent taking care of my younger sister. I never wanted to take care of her but there was no one else to do it. My older sister was away at College. I was denied the right from an early age to be a child to enjoy my adolescent years. The only fun time I had was when I was sent over to Devon's house to play. We never had much in common, but I was going through puberty and I enjoyed each moment we spent together. There are days I wish that I could relive my teenage years. No parent should take that from a child. Love and comfort should come first from within the home, if that cannot be found within the home; a child will go out in search of it. I felt neglected many times by my mother and most of the things I did as a child I did them out of desperation. The lack of love and attention from my mother made me vulnerable. I never wanted to be with a man, or encouraged any man to have sex with me; all I had yearned for then was love and attention. All I got in the end was abuse. Rape for me was not just the sexual act; it's more about dehumanizing my spirit and an abuse of my power and my privacy.

The months leading to the summer of my thirteenth birthday was filled with fun. I had to do an exam, which would put me in a specific class for my third grade, and I was waiting for school to finish. At the end of the school term, we were to go on a class trip, as most of us in the class would no longer become classmates the following year. I wanted so much to go on the trip. Seeing that I was already anti-social, it would be a great way of getting to know those I was around for two years. My mother as always made the cost of the trip a huge issue and I was denied the privilege of going on the trip. To this day, I still hold my mother responsible for allowing me to lose out on getting to know my classmates. My teacher Mrs. Fitzgerald tried everything she could to get me to go, but my mother said no. She gave me a choice between going on the trip and going to New York. Unfortunately, that summer I never got the visitor's visa to travel. I had one of the most boring summers of my life. The last days of summer 1993 changed my life; it brought me into a state of depression, a search for love and trying to find my identity, the person I ought to be. It was a focal point of my life where I realized that there is a thin line between love and hate.

4

A thin line between love and hate

"Boom bye bye in a batty boy head, rude boy nah promote no nasty man, them have fi dead".

—Buju Banton

Thirteen was a troubled year. I yearned for attention and I became more rebellious and more outspoken. Being a teenager was symbolic, as it was the gap between boyhood and manhood. I now had a mind of my own. I understood the world I was living in and I knew what society did to those who lived a socially unacceptable life in Jamaica. My culture was a living burden and the songs that were played personified the dialect and jargons and stigma towards sexuality. Nuff respect to Buju Banton, he is a musical legend and I love "Boom bye bye". The lyrics of "boom bye bye" will always be a part of Jamaica's dancehall cultural history. The song brought about huge controversy and became popular worldwide. The lyrics of dancehall music personify the taunting and violence towards homosexuals in Jamaica. It is normal for most reggae music to deal with the social concerns affecting Jamaica. Religion plays a fundamental role in Jamaica's cultural belief system and this is evident within most of the conscious lyrical sounds of reggae artistes.

It is important to clarify reggae music, dance hall music and that of raggae music. Music has always played a positive role in my life and reggae music without a doubt has been a true inspiration to me. I honestly think that the reggae music of the 60s, 70s, 80s and 90s cannot be compared to what these younger artistes are doing today. I am old school and I have the utmost respect for Bob Marley, Beres Hammond, John Holt, Gregory Isaacs, Ken Boothe, Dennis Brown and Freddy McGregor to name just a few. These men are conscious men who sing about real issues and they do not incite violence in the hearts of their listeners. The names I have listed above are reggae artistes and they have nothing in common with those of the dancehall music. It was Bob Marley who made reggae music into an international phenomenon with his chanting of love and peace. In the wake of Bob's success in the 1970s came a long host of noted names, and it wasn't long after that reggae became an established genre of music.

Reggae music has a long rich history, stemming long before Bob Marley was known on the international scene. Dancehall music and its chanting of more fire and an open condemnation of social taboo topics came about in the late 1970s. Jamaican music has its roots deeply embedded in its rich heritage of folk music, introduced by African slaves, influenced through contact with that of the white planter culture. The earliest form of noted Jamaican music was that of Mento, a simple folk calypso that emerged at the beginning of the 20th century as a variation to a dance derived from the French quadrille. Mento developed and became more popular during the 1940s and 1950s and became as popular as reggae is today. With the influence of the North American culture infiltrating the lives of most Jamaicans, mento gradually died out to the tunes of rock'n'roll in the 1950s.

Jamaicans added their own twist to rock'n'roll and created their own music, Ska. Ska was the first distinguishing style of music, reflecting the social consciousness of the time in Jamaica. Ska's birth is credited to the economically depressed areas of Kingston and it was adopted by the poor class of Jamaica who were feeling the aftermath of colonialism after independence from England. Though ska was short lived, it channeled elements from Jamaica's folk history. Ska had a profound impact on Jamaica who was at her infancy of independence. The island at the time was plagued with socioeconomic issues, and there was a growing discontent among the majority poor class. With the end of the ska era came about Rock Steady, which had angrier lyrics that reflected the changing times of the Jamaican society. To the poor mass music was all they had, to ease their pain of hard times and economic deprivation that was plaguing the island.

Rock Steady was the music of the people; it had a more conscious feel to it that encouraged the mass to have faith. It was during these time periods that Bob Marley and the Wailers came about. They were in tuned with the more conscious Rastafarian movement, who preached about repatriation. The Wailers were one of the few groups that had a moral, conscious message but it was their slow pace that got them more recognition. It is interesting to delve into the history of Jamaican music but this is not the forum. Rock Steady slowed down and gave way to a faster rhythm of music called Reggae music. While Rock Steady was short lived, much credit should be given to the Wailers, Joe Gibbs, Bunny "Striker' Lee, Delroy Wilson, Peter Tosh and Alton Ellis just to name a few. Reggae within itself is a unique cultural representation of Jamaica and its people and their spirituality. The music is strong and filled with power of assertion, self-identity and very much expressive of self. Reggae addresses more serious conscious issues of black self-determination. It was Bob Marley and the Wailers in the 1970s that brought reggae to the rest of the world. Sadly enough, reggae lost its momentum with the death of Marley in 1981 and Jamaica's conscious lyrics became modified. Dennis Brown and Freddie McGregor to name a few continued the musical tone that Bob left and it is still evident in the musical lyrics of Luciano.

Dancehall music emerged in the late 1970s and early 1980s with the slow pace of reggae music. Dancehall sprang from among Jamaican youths who were seeking a new focus in the music, it was still grass root but it personified something more closer to their hearts that included sex, drugs and dance. Dancehall music emerged from the streets of Jamaica with non-politically correct songs and pushed the limits of rude lyrical content of songs. While initially dancehall was never given public recognition, it was very popular among the masses as it could be heard at dance or popular street sessions. Sexually explicit lyrics were the brainchild of dancehall. With the advent of dancehall music came about DJ's who would propel the sounds of the dancehall era. Artistes such as Yellowman, Shabba Ranks (Godfather of the music) led the way for artist such as Beeniman and Bounty to now take center stage. Dancehall music became more and more popular as it spoke about social issues which were not socially acceptable, such as oral sex and homosexuality. While the music condemns sexual deviant practices, it personified the dons, drug dealers and the rude boy flex that also emerged out of the music. Most of Jamaican Dancehall singers are noted for their opposition towards homosexuals, while it is claimed that many of them are homosexuals themselves, so ironic!

Living in such an environment was nerve-racking. Many times I wanted to talk about my past and how I was feeling. The thought of being shut off by my family and even being beaten was too much, so I kept my thoughts to myself. It was not easy to fit into the cultural norm of what Jamaican culture defines as masculine.

Masculinity was defined by sexuality and how much of a good "fucka man" a man was. "Gal mi have mi hood in a you hole an mi nah teck it out", "Bombo red", "Position" "Punani too Sweet" were just a few songs that dealt with sexuality and the strength of a man in bed. Homosexuals had it hard but women had it much harder, if her man could not please her, it was unheard of for her to speak about it. Women had to face constant abuse by men during sex. Numerous women have been raped just in the name of masculinity. Penis was seen as a symbolic tool and it was used to oppress women and young boys. It was socially acceptable for a man to have more than one woman, as that was what men were expected to do. I knew what my culture stood for and I hated it but what was I to do, I have kept silent for all these years. I love my culture and dance hall music, I appreciate the music for what it represents to Jamaicans, but I detest the violence triggered towards women and homosexuals.

At any given dance in Jamaica, anti-gay lyrics are customary. The sound selector hypes the crowd to "bun a chi chi", "fire pan a batty boy", "all who no like batty man put up you han". Yes all hands would be up, even those who are gay. I lived my life in hiding and I would be one of the first to raise my hands up high, but now you would never get me to do that. When one talks about the violence portrayed at gays in a dance setting, one should not forget the violence portrayed at women also. One would ask if the women encourage these kinds of attitude, as they set the dress code of any given dance.

One of the main reasons Jamaicans hate homosexuals is because sex is used to define a man's strength and his level of masculinity. Sex is used as a weapon as a tool to dehumanize women and its so odd but women don't see it. Even those who understand the stigma do sleep with men who ill treat them. To be less of a man is to be a crime, and to not want to be in control of a woman is an even greater crime. Jamaicans see homosexuals as men trying to play the role of women, it's not about the emotions of two men being together, and it's more about the sexual act, the use of the penis which is seen in the eyes of Jamaicans as a weapon. Take for instance, the length of a man's penis tell how much of a man he is, the smaller the size of his penis the less of a man he is. With a small penis it is suggested that a man will be unable to please his woman, as all she desires is a huge penis. It comes back to the slavery issue, whereby black men were considered less of men because they had huge penis and thus small brains. That was the theory used to dehumanize men during slavery. Oddly enough, women felt more turned on by the huge penis size and derived more pleasure from it and hence the power play of the penis. Most tourists will tell you that they travel to Jamaica for a big 'bamboo', which is a large penis. That is all they think that Jamaica has to offer. So when a man leaves his manly duty of pleasing controlling a woman to be with a man, he must be condemned.

The "rude boy" attitude towards homosexual in Jamaica is so odd as in most instances it is the rude boy who is himself gay. One would expect that a rude boy would love women and love pussy, but that is far from the truth. It's all a front or what they call being on the down low or "DL" for short. Sure the rude boy is capable of pleasing his woman but his ultimate pleasure lies deep in the arms of a man. The concept DL is a universal concept and within the Jamaican context, they use the word "SPORT" to define themselves. These men do not associate themselves with the gay lifestyle, as they are all rude boys. I have seen too many of my friends who have a rude boy as his lover, and might I add he is not the one giving but more the one taking. There is something taboo about homosexuality and masculine men who associate themselves with the lifestyle. Another thing that attracts men to the homosexual life is insecurity about their penis size; this is as a result of cultural definition of black men and penis size. A black man with a penis size below seven inches feels very inadequate. Separate from the insecurity of the penis size, it's a huge turn on for some men to see a huge penis, as it represents strength and power and most men want to feel in control and it's a turn on to hold and feel another huge penis.

Beenie Man, Bounty Killa, Elephant Man, Vybz Kartel and other artist, while I love their music, they have no clue of the impact of their music as they incite the murder of gay people. Someone needs to take a stance and I am elated that the international community has taken a stance towards these artistes. Over the past few months gay-bashing dancehall stars have had concerts canceled in the UK, Belgium, Germany and the United States. Just recently Beenie man was banned from appearing at the MTV Video Awards concert held in Miami.

I recently had a chat with a artist, who finds trill in bashing homosexuals. It's ironic enough that he is Jamaican and gay. I did an interview with him, I won't call his name, but it was a most interesting chat.

David
Age: 27
Location: Jamaica
Occupation: Singer

"Why do you bash gays in your songs?"
"It's not necessarily bashing gays, its all the stigma attached to when you do consider yourself to be gay"
"Explain please?"
"Gay people are seen as flamboyant, loud, extremely promiscuous, its almost like the way we classify classes within society and its hard enough to be a minority and a black man and its much harder to be a gay black man."
"So are you saying you're condemning the lewd and flamboyant behavior we see in the Village in the City of New York?"
"Yes and no actually. There is a place and time for everything. In the Village which is a predominantly gay area, it's more acceptable as opposed to Church Ave and Flatbush in Brooklyn, New York."
"Its odd the way how you talk, as you yourself is a gay Jamaican a part of the dance hall community, you're like a hypocrite to yourself?"
"Not at all, as what I am to myself is a man, of masculine nature. I am very comfortable with my sexuality but I am even more comfortable with my masculinity. When surrounded by pagans you should not do what the pagans do. The bible says that we are in the world yet we should not be of the world."
"Man that is some bull, so are you gay or what?"
"NO"
"You're not gay but yet you have sex, or have sexual relations with men and you in your songs condemn those men who do the same things that you do, what is the difference with them being gay and you saying that you are not?"
"Now what I am is a free soul, I am very much not into labels; I am very much into females"
"Are you scared of the label or the word gay itself?"
"I am scared of the stigma attached to it. The guys who walk down Christopher street and act like women, and who try to be someone else, or feel as if they are trapped in a man's body because they get penetrated are Chi Chi man, and that is what I hate. One can still be gay and yet be a man, but its so hard, society see only one side of being gay and that is the flamboyant side of it, because it is so blatantly shown."
"Would you come out to your family or rather, your fans?"

"There is really nothing to come out to. In just the way I do not talk openly about the women I have sex with, why should I talk about my sexual encounters with men. I will not become an activist for the gay community. The Governor of New Jersey was not been an activist when he came out to the public was he?"
"So you're not a closeted gay man?"
"What does a gay closet look like?"
"Man you know what I mean"
"No I am a free soul as I told you, I have no inhibitions. I am just a man who struggles every day and I am who I am. A man who has sex with women only don't go out and introduce himself as straight, hell no he does not. So why should I label myself or hide in a closet."
"Well my good man, thanks for the insight, but I do think that you need to stop bashing gay men. I get your point about the flamboyant behavior, I don't support it myself, but it all boils down to respect."

It was an interesting conversation and I hope that more Jamaican artistes will have the guts to speak about why they hate gay men so much. I sometimes wonder if it's all about ignorance or somewhere during the socialization process they got hit on the head. I recently listened to one of Beenie Man's song bashing homosexual. If I were a child, I would want to act out on what was being said. Most times children believe what they hear or what they are told by adults. It's a much different thing for adults as they are more able to rationalize and reason for themselves but kids are impressionable. Beenie Man in one of his latest song advocates all manner of homophobic violence. Shooting is always the most common one, along with burning. The song goes like this. "'I'm dreaming' of a new Jamaica/come to execute all the gays.' But if that's too sophisticated for ya, get a load of this, from Batty Man Fi Dead: 'All batty man fi dead! From you fuck batty den a coppa and lead. Nuh man nuh fi have a another man in a him bed."

With words that incite violence what are we teaching the younger generation? It's hard to try to convince a child that he needs to be tolerant in a society where, so many songs are sung about gay men and that they should be killed. The Jamaican society sadly enough leaves no place in its cultural upbringing for differences. While censorship is quite popular among Jamaicans, the Government refuses to ban such lyrics from airplay, as they too condemn homosexuals on the island.

An interesting twist has occurred in the past few months regarding Corporate Sponsors in Jamaica. They are threatening to withdraw support from the local entertainment industry if dancehall artist continue to promote violence within their lyrics. In a joint statement in October 2004, Cable & Wireless Jamaica Ltd; Courts Jamaica Ltd; Digicel Jamaica, Red Stripe, Pepsi-Cola Jamaica and Wray & Nephew Ltd, said they would no longer lend their names to anything that incites or promotes violence. This open attempt by corporate Jamaica to use its economic power to rid the Jamaican music industry came in wake of the protest Outrage, A British-based gay activist group that has forced the cancellation of numerous reggae shows in Great Britain, which features such acts as Capleton, Beenie Man and Vybz Kartel.

While dancehall music personifies the rude boy image and endorses the "bad man" life style. There is a friend of mine who once told me of a gunman whom he was seeing and the way in which he reacted each time he came to his house late at night to get some good SEX. He was typical of any gunman in Jamaica who lives in the inner city and he is feared by any and everyone, as he is the "baddest bloodclath" man in town, yet he can't live without being "serviced". It's so ironic that he had enough women with whom he could have sex with, but there was just a different form of pleasure, a forbidden pleasure that could be derived from anal sex. If women were to understand the pleasure that can be derived from the prostrate, maybe more men would demand to be pleased by women and not men. The odd thing about the relationship my friend had with his gunman was that, the moment he ejaculated he became violent and the guilt of being with a man surfaces. It is never easy dealing with personal pleasure and the values that were instilled by our parents. Our parents tell us from a young age that being gay is wrong in the eyes of God. No one wants to displease God, but yet we know that within ourselves we see no wrong and that is where we find most of our sexual pleasures yet it is looked down upon by society.

5

Till Shiloh

○ ○
"I don't believe in failure, it is not failure if you enjoy the process".
—Oprah Winfrey

At the age of thirteen I lived through the eyes of my environment and upheld my cultural beliefs. I tried to keep my secret to myself but the burden was too much for me to bear. By the time I was in the third grade in high school my older sister was already in college and my younger sister was approaching her first birthday. I hated my little sister for being born. The love and attention that I had yearned for from my mother all these years were never to come to me. A young child needed them more than I. I played a fundamental role in the life of my younger sister. My mother was too caught up with her life and her business. It was hard enough dealing with my gay thoughts and it was even harder for me for all my free time was spent baby-sitting my younger sister. I lost my teenage years because of her and the fun of high school. I will never get the chance to live it ever again. I had developed a strong hatred towards my mother. I was once the baby boy and someone now took my spot. She never lived by the rule "two is better than two many". My younger sister is the jewel of my eyes and when she gets older I will apologize to her for how I ill-treated her as a child growing up.

The hatred I had for my mother escalated to numerous arguments and confrontations. I yearned for her attention but the struggles for her own survival made it worse. She too was in pain as she had yet a third child for another man who had claimed to love her, so we were both searching for comfort. I was the man of the house and I was my mother's right hand. I did it not for her. I did it to protect my sister. I never wanted her to be in a stranger's care for fear that she would have to undergo what I went through. I was a domesticated young man. I could cook; clean, wash, and iron but lacked the love of someone.

I had built-up anger for my mother and this anger led to us fighting. It was late one night and I was in my room preparing for a math exam. Math has always been my weakest subject. I was already in the top three of my class and in order to go to the top I had to excel in math. I was upset with my mother for her refusal to send me to extra class; she said there would be no one to spend time with my younger sister while she made money. My cousin and my sisters' best friend were at the house that night. I was asked in the middle of dealing with a difficult math problem to go to the shop for my mother's friend to purchase mosquito repellent. I was most upset; being the obedient child I did what I was told. I came back and I headed straight to my room, I was called again to give my mother water, she was next to the kitchen and could have done it herself but no she had to ask me. When I stood before her she spotted a pimple and decided to squeeze it. I was a teenager and I was suffering from bad acne. It was customary in my family that one of my grand aunts would do the honors to my uncles and get rid of their pimples. I sat while she did what she loved best and I started to cry. She asked me why was I crying and I told her that I had work to do and I am tired of her being in my face and she needed to spend the money and take me to a dermatologist to deal with my pimples. She informed me of what my aunt use to do to my uncles and I responded by telling her that if that was the case, "I don't want to be in the family". Who dared me to say such a thing? She turned around and slapped me twice in the face.

Now my mother is no small built woman, she is about 5'9" weighs about 195lbs and a strong built. She has thick firm legs, and heavy hands. She has a cocoa almond skin tone, short hair. She has bright eyes, small nose and thin lips like mine. She has the strength of ten lions and the voice of a dragon. She has a warm motherly feel to her and yet she possesses that rough Down Town Kingston mentality. In her own rights she can be a lady, but most people associate her with her loud mouth. Her foul language was like a second language. She is a bitch to be reckoned with and might I say apart from cursing she can fight like any man. She has a temper, which has some deep roots in her past, an anger that has not yet been let out. Apart from that entire bitchy vibes that she has at times, she still has a warm side to her. Most of her views in life I don't support; she is from the old school. She isn't practical in thinking. There is a Jamaican saying for children that say "you are to be seen and not heard" that is where she comes from. Sometimes she more than wanted to beat the black off me and my sister skin, she wanted to skin us alive.

The anger that I had built up for her was now open and I hit her back. My actions were so swift. I can hardly recall what happened within the short space of time. I clearly remembered us being in the front yard fighting, each blow she gave me I gave her one. It was just after 10pm and overcast as if it was going to rain. The thunder was rolling in the clouds, the stars were not visible that night, and it was as if the heavens were at war but no, it was my mother and I. It was a warm night and the wind was dry. I could hear the silence of the night. I could imagine that the neighbors could hear us out in the open of our yard. My mother is a rather boisterous woman so it would be no surprise for the neighbors to see her fighting. But for me and her to be fighting would be very odd. I was always a quiet child. I was sick of her attitude and I wanted it to end. I no longer wanted her for a mother. I remembered saying "I'm sick of your fuckery and I hate you" she cursed, I remember her cutting a stick from a plum tree in the front of the yard and she used it to beat me and those were some very heavy hits.

I have no clue what got over me that night but I had so much anger built up for my mother, that night I let it out and it may have come out the wrong way, but it changed my life. I can still remember the cutlass in my mothers' hand, my foot was cut, I had cut marks on my face and my right hand was bleeding. My shirt was torn off; my mother was almost without clothes. I had torn off her blouse and she was left in her bra. The skirt she had on was also torn and she had blood on her hands. I felt at one point that she was going to kill me but I was prepared to die that night. My mother was never a supportive mother and she held too much to her traditional belief of parenthood and she needed to stop. I felt abandoned by my mother, and my fear of abandonment has lived on with me even to this day. I have claimed to love but each time someone shows me love, I would begin to distrust him or her. I have been scared to be in a committed relationship, as I never wanted anyone to abandon me after loving them the way I loved my mother. She had no clue what comfort or love for a child meant, yet she had the gall to bring a third child into this world, I was most angry with that. Two is better than too many. Most men who abuse women will tell you that during their childhood they felt betrayed by their mother. A good number of men who have been sexually abused grow up to hate women as in most cases their mothers knew about the abuse and did nothing to protect them so these men have developed a continued distrust for women.

We had a trusted neighbor and she was called to intervene, thinking that I would have stopped, but I did no such thing. Yes, I never stopped hitting her until my neighbor was called in to separate us. Our neighbor was startled, as I was too quiet to commit such an act. My mother was determined to call the cops and my neighbor convinced her not to do it. She sat us both down and asked me to apologize but I refused to do it. My grandmother who lived in New York was called and she begged me to apologize, my mother told her that she was going to cut me off and no longer support me. My grandmother being the closest person in my life knew that I was troubled by something and decided to take me once more under her care. I told my mother sorry and I informed her that it never came from the heart. I did as my grand mother had asked me to do.

I went to bed that night crying and begging God to take my life, and if he did not, I was going to do it myself. I lashed out at my mother and rather than her asking me why I acted out she formed her own opinion and conclusion and the one person she should have ask why, she still up to this day have not asked me why. I have forgiven myself that night, as I never won the battle with my mother, as we both lived in two different worlds. It was now obvious that I had to go and find my own space to be me. I needed to talk to someone and I needed to find someone immediately. I spent many days at my neighbor's house; her nephew was now my newfound friend. I went to school the next day with the scars of the previous nights beating and yes I did fail the math exam. I never wanted to go home that day. My mother no longer spoke to me and I stop calling her mummy. She was now addressed as "Miss". I was given full independence. I was given all the keys to the house. She gave me little or no attention and I was called "sir". The resentment and alienation my mother gave me never made things better it brought me into a greater state of depression.

My troubles escalated much more as a few weeks later, my childhood playmate invited me over to his aunt's house, she was away in London and he said he had the house all to himself. I knew what he wanted; he wanted me to have sex with him. It was going to be my second time at it and even though I felt so much guilt after I f__ked him the first time, it was a huge comfort to do him again. It had rained the evening, and the grass outside was wet. The sky was now clear blue and there were no signs of white clouds and there was freshness in the air outside. It was late afternoon and after the rain the birds usually come out to chirp. It was a peaceful day but still not lovely enough to play out, just a day to relax and enjoy

God's creation. It was a Sunday and I had stewed chicken and rice and peas with carrot juice for dinner. When I went over to his aunt's house, I felt as if we were not alone but I was curious to know what was about to happen. The house was undergoing construction so it could have been a workman, but no, not a Sunday. I saw a pair of shoe at the front door and later on when I looked outside it was gone.

Mi was in the living room just a look in a deep space, cause mi did know say Something was about to happen, but how mi did a feel them last days mi would a entertain anything, even smoke weed, something mi neva do in a mi life. Mi fren did leave mi fi go bathe, him never teck long, him come out in less than ten minutes in a him brief.

CD players were a bit new to most Jamaican households and he decided to impress me by playing Buju Banton new CD *Til Shiloh*. I never liked it at first as it was moving away from the Buju we once knew, and he was singing more conscious lyrics.

Mi try mi best fi keep focus pan the lyrics but mi was more interested in what was about to happen. The window them in a di living room did half-open and the sun did a set outside. Mi could a see the colors of the sun outside from where mi was sitting; it had a red feel as if the sky was full of blood. On a more serious note mi did want something fi go bad that rass day, mi did fed up wid mi life, mi mummy and all that was around mi. Mi wish was about to come true.

Him come next to mi and mi fart, cause mi did nervous, and him start laughing at me. Him put in a dancehall CD and was dancing close to me, mi did a shake but mi was trying to keep mi cool. Mi did have on mi clothes still and then mi fren touch me. When mi look down pan him buddy, it did stan up stiff and then mi know wa him did want mi fi do. Him teck mi hands them and put it pan him buddy and then mine start getting stiff, mi never like the idea of touching him buddy but mi did like when him suck mi cocky and that was the only way it did ago start. Mi neva did a feel him up fi too long, then him walk out a di room and come back wid a bottle of lotion and a towel. Them days we nevea did know bout KY nar lube, all we had was lotion or coconut oil. As always he was the lead, him lay the towel pan the carpet and put the lotion in a him batty and hold on to mi cocky. Him did kneel down and tell mi fi come behind him. Him hold on to mi cocky and teck him time and put mi cocky in a him, him did tight no rass, but it did feel sweet. This was the second time mi did a fuck him, an though it was with a man, it did still feel sweet. Honestly mi neva did know say mi would a fuck a bwoy before mi fuck pussy, but ya know fuck a fuck. Him did love the way mi brace the cocky in a him, him did a cry but him never did want mi fi stop, fi some reason him seem to love it more than mi. Him did tight and most times it did kind a hard fi put it all di way in, but mi stop when him did start fi bleed as mi hate fi see blood. Mi tell him say mi ago stop and when mi teck it out him tell mi fi jerk off and cum pan him chest.

After mi cum there was the usual silence and then we just put on back we clothes wid out saying a word to each other. Fa some reason while mi did a fuck him it did feel like say somebody did a watch mi, mi could a feel a strong energy and yes mi was right. Mi neva have a clue who it was but mi did fi later find out say mi playmate, the same bwoy who re-introduce mi to the batty boy life made a bet wid him cousin, say mi would fuck him and let him watch fi money. Later on mi find out say the bet was fa more than money, it was something else but right now mi no rememba.

I went back home feeling empty, as if I had done something wrong. Something inside me told me that this was the end of my friendship with my friend, and deep within I felt betrayed by what I had thought he had done to me. I went home and took another shower as I now felt dirty, it was unsafe and oddly enough I wanted to cut my penis off. I went into a state of depression that night and I prayed to God asking him to forgive me once more. I never saw myself as being gay but I felt as if I had committed an act against God. I used to sing on the church youth choir and I had felt the Holy Spirit many times and I was saved by the blood of God. I went as far as to be baptized and re-confirm my commitment to God. I prayed to God for a healing potion, something to drink or even a pill to take, to take the thoughts away. The acts that I had committed with my friends confirmed in my mind that I was gay, but I knew that there was a God in heaven and he alone answers prayer and he could heal me. That week I was in church on my knees, crying and giving God all the praise, as I felt there was a demon inside of me and I needed to let him out, let him loose and allow God to set my soul free. God never answered my prayer and I found out that there is no demon inside of me, and I am not cursed, I am a child of God and he loves me unconditionally.

A week and a half later, my friend came back to my house not for me to have sex with him, but because his cousin wanted to talk to me. I never declined and I took my bold self and went to the cousin. The cousin told me all that he saw and told me that he was going to tell my family. I informed him that he would be in more trouble than I would if he did. My family would send me far away and he would have been killed or something bad would have happened to him. He knew the person my mother was and he feared her wrath so, he apologized and a friendship was formed that night. He felt sorry for what he had done and wanted me to forgive him. I had cut off communication with my childhood friend and his cousin now became the person I could sit and talk to and tell him my inner most thoughts and secrets. I had dreams and he took his time out to listen to me, he encouraged me to do well in school and my grades got even better. While I did love the man who raped me, the man who had taken my virginity, pop my cork, I refuse to put life to him or even meaning to his existence. Call me bitter, yes I am, and I have all right to. Throughout the entire book I will refer to my abuser as 'Him' or "He".

6

Men in pain

○ ○

I'm A man

"She washed my penis rolling it around in her hands
I feel aroused.
She puts her lips on it kissing, gently sucking
I feel it growing.
After all, "I'm a Man." I should be enjoying this.
Does it matter that
I haven't turned two yet?"
—*Unknown*

When I was in college I read an article about Oprah Winfrey who stated that she was sexually abused as a girl. I later heard her say it herself but I still did not believe. Oprah, damn! She is the Queen of talk and a diva in her own rights and even if something like that happen to her why would she want to talk about it publicly. I felt that only poor people got molested, as they had to share beds with six or more people so it was inevitable that they would be sexually abused. Further more, Oprah is rich why would she want to say all this and to the public at that. I later realized that it was a healing process and the more you talk about the abuse openly, candidly and publicly the more you realize that it was not your fault. It was Oprah's openness to share with the world her pain that prompted me to speak out about my abuse and come to terms that it was not my fault.

I was living on a tiny island and I was afraid of the consequence of telling anyone what happened to me. As I got older and started reading more on human sexuality I found out for myself that men can also be victims of sexual abuse. "The rape of men in our communities is perhaps the most underreported and un-addressed violent crime. The intense shame and stigma attached to adult male rape arguably exceeds that of rape of women…" *Male on Male Rape: The Hidden Toll of Stigma and Shame*—Michael Scarce.

I am not trying to argue that men find it more difficult to cope with sexual abuse, but male survivors often have an especially difficult time revealing that they were abused. The effects of sexual abuse are equally profound whether the victim is male or female. There are certain similarities but the consequences are literally the same. It is however, my opinion that men and boys find it a bit more difficult to come to terms with the fact that they were sexually assaulted. It wasn't until late in my life, actually while living in the United States that I realized that men and boys could be raped on such a frequent basis. "Sexual abuse does not lessen a woman's worth or a man's maleness. Like being robbed, SEXUAL ABUSE IS A CRIME AGAINST YOU, NOT AN INDICATOR OF WHO YOU ARE."

In researching sexual abuse of men and boys in Jamaica, the Government had no distinction of the cases reported by men or boys as even in the case of abuse they are never reported out of shame and embarrassment. I was met with bureaucracy and circumvolution by the Government and led from one organization to the other which to this day has not been able to give me any information of substance. I can't believe that in this day and age the Government is still in denial that homosexuality exists in the country. I hope before I die that someone will conduct a study on the abuse of men and boys in Jamaica.

When men are sexually abused they live constantly with a sense of confusion about their sexuality. "Since the abuse was committed sexually, it is often mistakenly seen as an act of sexual passion instead of what it really is—an aggressive, destructive violation of another human being",—Mike Lewis, *Victims No Longer: Men Recovering from Incest and Other Sexual Child Abuse 1986*. When a boy or man is sexually abused by another man, most times it is erroneously seen as a homosexual act. It cannot be considered a homosexual act, as it was not done with consent; it was an act of force. One of the main reasons why Jamaican men and young boys refuse to speak openly about abuse is as a result of society confusing the sexual act as a homosexual activity. An act of homosexuality does not make a person a homosexual. How can a society also blame the victim? It is the individual who committed the crime that should be wronged. No means no and abuse is abuse no matter what form it takes.

Like me, many boys and men who are victims of sexual abuse are faced with confusion about their sexuality and often times consider themselves to be homosexuals. It becomes even more complicated when a boy is sexually abused by a woman. Sexual activities between older women and young boys are rarely seen as abuse in the Jamaican society. It is considered a right of passage and it is somewhat encouraged. The sexual acts in most cases are ignored and the young man is seen as gay if he complains about the continued sexual abuse. "Being victimized by a woman appears to bring an added level of shame; men are more likely to blame themselves or discount it as not really being abuse...If we are to effectively deal with incest, we must create a climate that recognizes all sexual abuse for what it is. Incestuous abuse is harmful regardless of the gender of the perpetrator or the victim."—Mike Lewis, *Victims No Longer: Men Recovering From Incest and Other Sexual Child Abuse 1986.*

Men and boys who are victims of sexual abuse will continue to be in pain and denial unless as a society we confront the myths of manhood. What we need to do is to support those who have been victimized by rape regardless of sex and hold accountable those who do the victimizing. Perhaps repelling the homosexual laws in Jamaica may be a step in the right direction to prevent continued abuse of both men and boys. If the country allows men to be free and be themselves, maybe when frustration and the desire to act on their homosexual feelings set in, these men would not attempt to molest young boys as they would be free at will to practice their lifestyle.

The stories of two young men have influenced my life like no other personal experience. I find both stories inspiring as they are both young boys, it also shows to the world the horrible effects of sexual abuse of young boys.

The first story is that of a young seven-year-old boy. I read his story in a local paper. I can't recall the date. The article stated, as I remembered it, — the young boy was very jovial and friendly and all of a sudden he became withdrawn and distant. His mother thought of it as a phase, as boys were never socialized to show emotions so he was just becoming a man and not dealing with the real issues around him. His mother had to take the young boy for a physical and it was there the doctor found out that the young man was torn at his anal opening. The doctor questioned the child about what happened and eventually he told the doctor what happened. The article stated that the young boy was left at school to be picked up one afternoon and his mother took longer than expected. The young boy was left in the care of the security guard at the school and it was he who raped him. As gross as it sounds one would wonder what an older man could find pleasurable by having sex with an innocent, defenseless child, but that question only a molester and rapist could answer, as the question still lurks in my head even today. The doctor had no choice but to tell the mother who did the unexpected. She went to the school the following day and confronted the security guard. It was daylight and school was still in session and her son was also at school. By the end of the school day the young child had felt the full brunt of his mother's actions. Children can be cruel and they teased him about the rape and called him a faggot, and a "batty man". He was too young to cope with what was going on and his mother could not comfort herself and was unable to comfort her own child and give him emotional support. A few days later he was found dead, he hung himself at age seven. Each time I relate his story, my eyes are filled with tears as it hurts to see how a mother could be so cruel and that is one of the reasons I took so long to tell my mother.

The second story is that of a twelve-year-old boy, who lived with his single father. His mother for some reason was never mentioned in the article but I believed she was dead. The young boy was being interviewed and he was telling his story of how his father raped him from age seven until he was in his late teenage years. He told his story with the utmost innocence. He remembered the first time his father touched him, he was only seven years old and he was taking a shower and his father touched him on his penis. He said it became more intense when he was going through puberty and his father realized that he had an erection. He said early one morning his father came into his room and gave him oral sex, he said it felt odd but he enjoyed the feeling. He said his father never spoke to him after the acts were committed and he was also expected to give his father oral sex. He saw nothing wrong with it as it was seen as a form of bonding. He told the reporter that he never had sex with his father until he was fourteen and even though it hurt, he was with his father so what was he to do about it. He said that he found comfort in having a girlfriend and having sex with her regularly. The thought of telling anyone what his father was doing to him hurt too much and the thought of loosing him killed a part of him so he kept it a secret for years.

I was not much different from this boy, I felt trapped and I felt as if I had nowhere to escape to. The first thing in healing is to admit that it was not your fault. Adults are there to protect you and should not take advantage of their power of authority. As I got older, I met young men my age and older who have been through similar situations like me and there were others who have been through much tougher experiences. Some of these men still reside in Jamaica and a good number of those I know who have been molested, have run away from Jamaica never to return. Like me, most of these men have not dealt with the pain of rape or molestation. The anger in most cases is still curled up deep inside them, waiting for the moment or the wrong person to lash out at them for them to maybe, commit some heinous crime. The act alone does not make you homosexual, but in a society that condemns even victims of homosexual acts, who would want to talk up or speak out about such a horrible act of violence. I grew up, reading and hearing about the beatings and killings of young men and grown men, who are homosexuals. The stories are so horrific; it ensures us victims that its best to keep our mouths shut and live with the pain until death do us part.

In doing this chapter I posed a question to the general chat room in go-jamaica.com/chat. The question was, can a woman rape a man or a young boy? Almost everyone in the room said that it was impossible for a woman to rape a man. Some argued that one cannot rape the willing, because rape can only occur when there is penetration. The general consensus of the room at the end was that a woman cannot rape a man. A few suggested that it could happen, but the fact that the man had an erection could be in question. (Questions and responses can be found in Chapter 7) The realty of life however is, yes, women do sexually abused boys and can also rape a man. Ann Cossins in *Masculinities Sexuality and Child Abuse* argues that, Feminism has been criticized for ignoring the evidence that shows that boys are also victims of child sexual abuse. Cossins further claims that a significant proportion of the perpetrators of boy child abuse are female. She argued further that non-feminist research over the years have ignored or dismissed the possibility that women could have a sexual interest in children or that it would be possible to engage in sexual abuse without a penis.

After reading Cossins article the first thing that came to mind was the movie *Antoine Fisher* that I recommend to each reader. A female sexually abused Fisher while in foster care and it haunted him for years. It had a profound impact on how he related to women. It is clear based on studies that child sexual abuse by females do occur even without penetration. It is important to note the double standards within feminist research as they argue with no empirical data, that the vast majority of child sexual offenders are male and the vast majority of victims are female. I wonder what world these feminists live in. I believe in equality of the sexes but while fighting to be equal, feminists needs to understand the nurturing role of motherhood and live up to that responsibility first. As women and mothers, they need to lower the bar that is set to define masculinity. Maybe if we teach our boys how to be themselves and stop placing them in a role from a young age maybe they would be more open to speak about sexual abuse.

Fortunately, I had spoken to three young men who had promised to give their personal experience about sexual abuse and how it has affected their lives and how their families dealt with it. They are all Jamaicans, two reside in the US and the other currently resides in Jamaica. Their stories have uplifted me. I hope these men will find the strength to forgive themselves and even though I have opened a wound by opening up the discussion of sexual abuse, they were brave enough to share them with me. I hope that whoever read this book, whether they live in Jamaica or outside of the island will start having conversations with their child or children. For those who are victims of abuse take the time to talk to someone about your experience. As a family, as a community we need to break the cycle, it takes one person to make a difference. The family is one of the most important institutions and its main function is to protect and love. Our men are in pain, their anger is hurting all of us, when will we put a stop to all this madness? These are the stories of men in pain.

Gregory
Age: 19
Location: Brooklyn NY
Occupation: Escort

"I have lived a f__ked up life, look at me man, I am just nineteen and I look much older than my age. I feel like an old man of about forty trapped in the body of a boy. My cousin f__ked me when I was about ten years old, and I will never forget that night, but I would not consider it to be rape. We were both young and we were home alone watching porn. I got hard; he was jerking himself and one thing lead to another. It might sound sick, him being my cousin and all but it was mad cool. I felt that I had to let him penetrate me as he was the older one and I know he would not let me do him. I am the thirteenth of fourteen kids and when I got to the United States I was unfortunately put into the foster care system, because my mother was unable to take care of me. Those boys, at the home raped me, they f__ked me good and it has made me a tougher man to this day. I still see them around my way, they claim that they not gay but they are gay. I don't even know if I am gay, I just love f__king niggas. The good part about it, I don't have a job and it pays my bills. Nigga don't want no bytch, they just fronting, they want a nigga to f__k them hard and rough. I never wanted to be an escort, it just happened. It was this cat I was fucking with, and he introduced me to a friend of his and it started paying me good so I made it into a profession.

I am not there when I am with a nigga, it's just my dick, my body is there but my mind is somewhere else, it's not all that serious. I still love my girls, but this is just what I do. I have learned so much from this gig, I have traveled to so many states, f__ked so many niggas, I should be rich by now, but I was foolish. There is this one Jamaican man, from Atlanta who would fly me down to his home whenever his wife was out of town and, and pays well. For that one weekend I can make as much a three grand. He gives me his car to drive and he tells his friends that he is my mentor. I don't consider myself to be gay, as I am not in the life.

Honestly, I am in pain, I smoke weed a lot, just to clear my mind, just to put something's in the back of my mind, as it's just too much to deal with. Most niggas want to f__k me because I am so slim and I have a tight body, but that can only happen when I am drunk or high. Sometimes I wish I could live my life over again, but I am an old soul and everything happens in life for a reason. I am in school, I do music, and one day I hope to become a professional singer. I don't want you to think that escorting is all I do, but most times it's all I got. Many of these guys who are young like my self do get rape on the job, by groups of men, but them niggas will never f__k with me as I can always reason on their level. I know I need help, but it's just too much. Big man, I am def. going to buy a copy of your book, as we need to talk about these things, but are we ready to deal with it."

Robert: 28
Location: St. James, Jamaica
Occupation: Technician

I wasn't able to convince Robert to write in his own words his story as he said he could not find the words to express himself. Robert is 28 years old and I met him while searching in a Jamaican chat room. Robert has a girlfriend and a young son and they all reside in Montego Bay.

Often on the weekend Robert would leave his son with his mother in the country and he would spend a bit of quality time with his wife to be. They usually go to a hip club on the hip strip of Montego Bay then walk along the beach before returning home. While the crime rate is relatively high, he felt safe as he grew up in that parish all his life and was never a victim of crime.

Late one night at about 11pm, after leaving a restaurant both Robert and his girlfriend decided to go clubbing and decided to go home and spend the night watching television. They took a cab; there were only four people in the cab including the driver. Close to the end of the journey the passenger next to them held them both at gunpoint and then the driver deterred off the main road onto a lonely dark road, it was apparent that the driver was in on the robbery. Robert gave the men all of his cash and all the jewelry both he and his girlfriend had but they wanted more.

They tied his girlfriend up and led her aside. The unimaginable happened to Robert he was gun butted in the head and was forced to perform oral sex on one of the men. He was later held down and raped by the other man who was the robber. His girlfriend was never harmed. It was a life and death situation so it was either he allowed them to have sex with him or be killed. (I wanted to know details but he refused to, but I could imagine). They both went home that night in silence, she knew what happened to him and to this day they have not spoken about the incident.

This occurred two years ago. Robert intends to marry his girlfriend at the end of 2004 but is scared that at one point in the marriage they would both have to deal with the past but he is still not ready to deal with it. The problem is, he still enjoys sex with his girlfriend but there is something in his mind that is telling him that he needs to explore sex with men. I have strongly suggested against this idea, as I believe that before he do attempt to explore he should first get help. Though he has not yet acted on the desire he is not far from doing do. He is scared most of all from getting professional help, as he does not believe that he is sick. The last time I spoke to him I reminded him that he has a son and he should get help even not for himself but for his child as his unresolved issues could destroy his family. I told him that he is no where close to being gay and that he started the healing process by telling me his story but he needs to take a step further and get help. He has my information and on occasion makes contact but he is doing well.

Travis
Age:25
Location: New York
Occupation; Administrative assistant

Many gay men have asked me the dreadful question that pertains to the time in my life when I recognized that I had feelings for men, but there was never a time that I could provide them with an accurate answer. I say dreadful because it is one of those questions that just seem unanswerable. Anyways, I would say that as my teenage year drew to a close, I began to identify certain factors in my life that most people would describe as gay tendencies. Some of these factors include my passion for shopping, fashion, decorating and the list goes on. My behavior in my school locker room was also synonymous with that of a gay person, in the sense that I would pick out the guys that were handsome, muscular and sexy and tended to start conversations with them. Mainly I wanted to scrutinize their "package" as it was a turn-on. I also enjoyed being wrestled to the ground during my lunch hour and participating in "homo-erotic" sports such as basketball, where every time I scored, one of my teammates would slap my ass cheek. Who would not like that? Well, those were my high school years and I began to align my being with homosexuality. Yet, I could sense inner turmoil. A struggle between good and evil, so what society considered evil, i.e. homosexuality. But not just society, more over religion. I was an active "church boy" and we all know what that means. I was the ideal church member at 15, 16, 17, and on. I knew all the stories in the Bible and could recite most, if not all. I sang in the choirs and enjoyed Men's Retreat. Yeah, Men's Retreat, where all the young men of the church came together to fellowship and pray in a secluded location miles away from the church building. This was another opportunity to check out the "brothas" and ironically, to be checked out by others, as I would come to learn.

My first encounter with a man was at Men's Retreat and no we were not praying. I was invited to one of the evangelist's room to talk about anything that was on my mind. I could tell based on his mannerisms and tone, he was sexually interested in me. So I went and that's when I had my first kiss. We fondled each other for a short period of time as I was scared and too naïve especially I felt how well endowed he was. He did not attempt to have sex with me, which I thought was very respectful given my obvious nervousness. We had no other sexual contact throughout the duration of the retreat.

Living in a country like Jamaica and being a member of my family was not the easiest thing for me as an up and coming gay man. Other than the evangelist, no one else knew that I was gay. The people in Jamaica are extremely homo-phobic. I was extremely fearful of anyone even getting the idea that I was gay. Now that I write about it, I think I was more fearful of the spiritual repercussions i.e. not being able to go to Heaven as a result of my sin and how it pertains to the Sodom and Gomorrah's story in the Bible. I almost felt as though I had a decision to make in terms of choosing a lifestyle, one that would be conducive to biblical righteousness. Yet, until today I still struggle with this.

Migrating to the US was probably the most beneficial thing for me as a gay man, as I was more comfortable to engage in sexual relations with other men and to actually pursue a relationship. I had a few, some up and others down. Again I was more comfortable with who I am, although I would not be caught in a gay club or even the gay area of town.

My mom never suspected that I was gay because in her eyes I was her perfect son. I was an A student, who had a girlfriend, who she thought was wonderful and she saw the potential for a future between us. Having a girlfriend was difficult because deep down I knew I could not love her as I would a man. In other words, I felt I emotionally neglected to care for her. During this time, I had a close friend who I messed around with from time to time. When I say mess around, I mean kiss, cuddle, and the likes, nothing major sexually. Eventually, I walked out of my girlfriend's life because I was tired of lying to her and myself. That did not go over too well, but that I can discuss at some other time, not now. Nonetheless, we both moved on with our lives.

Church here in the US for me was better because homosexuality seemed to be tolerated to some extent. Yet, that was no motivation for me to come out of the closet. Nothing was at this point in my life simply because too many things and relationships were at stake. I was not prepared to lose any. They were my support networks. I cannot imagine life without them. But I was also scared about how God viewed my life and me. Was my praise still pleasing in His sight? Would I still be able to fulfill His will? Will I still be a chosen vessel? I am still on an ongoing quest to find the answers to those questions. I believe that there will come a day when they are answered.

I had a terrible relationship experience and it was at that point that I had to tell my mom, whom I was so very close with that I am gay. I knew she would handle the information and she did. Maybe not emotionally well at first, but she did and now we are much closer than we ever was. I love my mom and she loves me gay or straight, as if sexuality should ever come between a mother and a son. Sadly, it does. I thank God for my mom. Mom is the only family who knows and it will be that way for a while. Mom says it is my business and why should I publicize it…it is my sex life for God sakes.

Well, life goes on. Here I am today and I love my life as it is. I am a gay male who has been extremely successful. Being gay did not restrict me from earning a bachelor's degree, a master's degree, beginning my career, buying a house and a car, singing in my church choirs, and becoming involved in my local community activities. The only downfall to my life is that from time to time I feel like I am deceiving some of my friends, coworkers and family members who have no clue I am gay. But is it really deception? They did not tell me they were straight, but I assumed. To be quite honest I do not care whether or not they love people of the same gender. More power to them if they do, join the club. I still worry about God and I and what will happen in the end, but I pray that His grace and mercy will be sufficient to the very end.

One of the problem with many men, whether gay or straight is that they lack trust. So currently I am single and still searching for one I can love and who can love me. I hope he comes with honesty and a strong supportive spirit because this life of being gay is not the easiest, although such is life whether gay or straight. Yeah, the struggle continues and I am happy either way. I love being gay and I am happy with my life. For those who do not, it is too bad because you are only putting yourself at a disadvantage, since there is more to me and to other men than simply being GAY.

7

Chi Chi Man

> "My Crew (My Crew) my dogs (My dogs)
> Set rules (Set rules) set laws (set laws)
> We represent for di lords of yards
> A gal alone a feel up my balls
> Chorus:
> From dem a par inna chi chi man car
> Blaze di fire mek we bun dem!!!! (Bun them!!!!)
> From them a drink inna Chi Chi man bar
> Blaze the fire mek we dun dem!!!! (Dun dem!!!!)"
>
> —TOK

In order for you, the reader to understand why young men refused to speak out against their abusers, you will have to understand the culture of Jamaica, the general attitude of the population and the Government at large. The quote above reflects a popular song that encourages the killing of gay men. Seeing that the Jamaican society defines homosexuality by the sexual act, if I were a boy I would keep my mouth shut about being sexually abuse. I am not here to justify or condemn homosexuality, as I don't care what two grown adult males do in the privacy of their home that is their prerogative not mine. As a victim of sexual abuse I need to bring to the table some of the cultural reasons why Jamaican men who have being sexually abused refuse to admit to the reality of the abuse and how society forces them to keep quiet indirectly.

This is an unedited chapter. I have listed some sexual offenses, their definitions and sentencing based on information posted on the web site of "*The Center for*

Investigation of Sexual Offenses and Child Abuse (C.I.S.O.C.A), established on December 1st, 1998 within the Community Relations Branch of the Jamaica Constabulary force. The listing will clearly show that there is nothing in the Jamaican written laws that protect the rights of boys who have been sexually molested. The current laws on the table are outdated and need to be reconstructed to fit into contemporary Jamaican society. I have taken articles from the Jamaican news media that reflects the general attitude of the cultural beliefs of Jamaicans towards homosexuality. The articles are all current. You the reader will read for yourself, how Jamaicans view homosexuality, how the government views it and also how the church will tackle the subject. I have also enclosed the unedited versions of interviews conducted by young men who have never been sexually abused but asked the question what they would do if they were sexually assaulted.

C.I.S.O.C.A
Some Sexual offenses, Their Definitions and Sentencing
Incest

Incest is having sexual intercourse with a biological (blood) relative and is committed when any male person has sexual knowledge of his mother, daughter or sister, or where a female person permits her grandfather, father, son or brother to have carnal knowledge of her. NB. If a female 16 years and over knowingly permits a blood relative to have sexual intercourse with her, she too can be charged with incest. That is, (Son, father, and grandfather).

Sentencing:—one. Incest By male

Sec. 2(1) Any male person who is found guilty of committing incest, is liable to be imprisoned for up to five years. If it is alleged and proved that the female is under age of twelve years, the offender can be sentenced to a maximum of 10 years in prison with hard labor.

Sentencing:-two. Incest By female of or over sixteen

Any female person sixteen years or over, who consents to an incestuous relationship if convicted in court, is liable to be imprisoned with hard labor for a term not exceeding five years.

Indecent Assault

Indecent Assault includes any touching or fondling of the "private" parts of the body (breast, genital area, or buttocks) of another. In the circumstances, the offender knows that the conduct is likely to cause embarrassment.

Sentencing

Persons found guilty of Indecent Assault upon any female or attempts to have carnal knowledge of any girl between 12 and 16 years, is liable to imprisonment of up to 3 years at hard labor.

Buggery

Buggery is committed by anyone who has anal intercourse with any human being or animal or any woman who has any sexual intercourse with animal.

Sentencing

Persons convicted of buggery, committed either with a human being or animal, is liable to imprisonment with hard labor for up to ten years.

Rape

Rape is the use of physical force, fear or fraud in obtaining sexual relations with a woman against her will and without consent. For rape to be proven, penetration must take place.

Sentencing

Persons found guilty of rape can be sentenced to life imprisonment.

Carnal Abuse

Carnal abuse is having unlawful carnal knowledge of a girl under the age of sixteen (16) years.

Sentencing: one

Anyone who is convicted of an attempt to have carnal knowledge of any girl under the age of twelve years is liable to imprisonment of up to ten years.

Sentencing: two

Anyone who has sexual intercourse with any girl above the age of 12 years old and under age 16 years old shall be guilty of misdemeanor and if convicted, be liable to imprisonment for a period not exceeding seven years.

Assault with Intent to Rape

Attempting rape is where penetration may have taken place but cannot be proven. The victim may have been unconscious and wakes up to see a man with an erect penis standing over her.

Sentencing

A person convicted of attempted rape is liable to imprisonment for a period of up to seven years.

Articles
Youthlink
Jamaica.com
Sexual Orientation/Crime On the Island

"Has Jamaica become another Sodom. Seem like Jamaica had adopted too much from abroad as far as sexual preference etc.,

As a returning resident I feel like I'm in Atlanta Georgia and that's definitely Sodom. What has become of little Jamaica. Why are we picking up the things that a place in the US has left behind?

I believe Jamaica crime rate is higher than New York now. As they had done a massive clean up there.

What are we teaching our children here? Men sleeping with men, women with women, men and women sleeping with children. No wonder the spread of AIDS is so rampant. and cannot be contained.

We as citizens of this country need to start working together to combat these things.

What do you think??????
Carol Boothe"

The Jamaican Observer
Father encourages students to maul 'gay' son at Dunoon Tech
Police also stoned in school riot

By Karyl Walker Observer staff reporter
Thursday, February 19, 2004

"In notoriously homophobic Jamaica gay men can hardly expect protection even from their parents—as was made very clear yesterday.

A father, concerned that his son might be gay, turned up at the Dunoon Park Technical High School in East Kingston and apparently encouraged other students to beat the boy, an eleventh grader.

"Them Bruck up desk and bench and beat him up badly," one Dunoon student told the Observer. "Him get nuff lick, box, kick and thump from boy and girl."

The boy's name was withheld by school officials and the extent of his injuries was not immediately known. But whatever they were, it would have been worse were it not for the intervention of an ancillary staff.

According to students and teachers at the school, the boy's father apparently found pictures of nude men in the boy's school bag.

Infuriated, he turned up at the school yesterday with the pictures and encouraged the mob to turn on his son. As students began to maul his son, the man is reported to have driven away.

In the frenzy, students hurled stones at the police who were called to the school to restore order; in the process damaging police cars and motorbikes. The police eventually were able to rescue the youngster from the other students, most of whom wore uniforms, and whisked him off the campus. According to teachers at the school, people from outside the school joined in the fracas.

"They were intent on killing him," this teacher said. "They were like a pack of wild animals who had smelled blood and if it wasn't for a staff member who jumped on top of him, you would be reporting on a mob killing." the teacher described the behavior of the father as "careless".

"A me save him," an ancillary staff member told the observer. "Me have to jump on him and shield him cause them was going to kill him. Me get whole heap of licks, but me push him in the office and lock him in."
School authorities were forced to call the Elliston Road police to escort the boy off the compound when the angry mob became uncontrollable.

But the cops were also attacked, leaving some with minor injuries. After calm was restored, at least a dozen Dunoon students were taken to the Elliston Road police station where they were given a stern warning by officers from the station's Criminal Investigation Bureau before being released."

The Jamaican Observer
Homosexuality is wrong

Thursday, December 04, 2003
Dear Editor,

"There is no way homosexuality could be deemed right, godly, and wholesome or whatever else you all want to call it. Homosexuality speaks tot he fact that they are born the way they are and it is their right to be the way they are.

They are perfectly correct, we are born homosexuals, murderers, thieves, and with all forms of evil thoughts on our minds; even to commit bestiality.

One of the greatest things that is preventing us from doing al that we think is within out right to do or that we were born to do is the whole matter of choice. We can chose to be homosexuals, thieves, to commit incest, molest children whatever.

Since homosexuals speak of the right to do what they want to do, then the murders, rapist, thieves and child molesters have a right to do what they want since they too were born this way. Don't you think?

If it were that all men should choose other men as partners, where does procreation come in?

It is interesting to note that the church is encouraging this kind of behavior, because if I read my Bible correctly, Sodom and Gomorrah were destroyed for that very act of Sodomy (among other things, of course). The church above all else should realize that (that is, if the church believes in God, is worshipping the same God we talk and know about) the devil has certainly found the root of "vine" (the church) to spread this kind of deception.

Last but not least, if it is that a man finds it necessary to have sex the way he does, why choose a man to do so with, he can do it the same way with women, if they allow it!

I know this will not stop homosexuality from being who they choose to be, but please do not try to justify your carnal act by saying nonsense and that your act of homosexuality is all right.

In fact, dogs don't do it; other animals don't, so why, with all our so-called intelligence, we are going against the laws of nature?

I'll tell you, though; it cannot be right by any standard, given the facts.

J Morrison

The Jamaica Gleaner
Special Feature
Homos at Risk

July 25, 2001

"Homosexuals are increasingly becoming the targets of hate crimes in Jamaica but are afraid to press charges against their assailants for fear of bringing attention to their lifestyle.

This, according to a number of human rights advocates, is a result of the homophobic nature of the society where the vilification of gays has always been the norm. In a statement sent to the Gleaner, Jamaica Forum for Lesbians, All-Sexuals and Gays (J-FLAG) said that the group was deeply distressed by reports of attacks on people island-wide that were alleged to be homosexuals. It noted that the incidents exemplified some of the challenges, which gays and lesbians encounter on a daily basis.

"Any act of discrimination meted out to an individual known or alleged to be gay, lesbian or all sexual is inhumane and intolerable," the statement read. "Moreover, it is a blatant violation of human rights as outlined in Articles of the Universal Declaration of human rights and the Jamaican Constitution."

Earlier this year, several students attending the Northern Caribbean University in Mandeville were attacked and beaten for alleged homosexual involvement. There is also the case of a man, suspected to be gay, who last year was shot and killed on the steps of a church in Kingston. Even within the high schools, students who are deemed to be too effeminate are the victims of hate crimes.

"Kids can be merciless," explained one principal who requested not to be identified in the story. "I have had to both suspend and expel students for brutally beating up on other schoolmates believed to be homosexuals. Sometimes even the taunting can be vicious. I have spoken to principals of other schools and they also have similar experiences with their students."

The police, too, are aware of some of the attacks, which have been made on gays but note that they hardly have enough evidence to go on. Several months ago in St. Catherine, police officers had to rescue two men from being killed by a group of angry residents. The men were allegedly caught having oral sex in the back seat of a car.

"Yes, it is something that happens quite frequently," explained an officer attached to the Montego Bay police station. "Homosexuals are afraid to report some of the atrocities that have been carried out against them for fear of being exposed so they remain quiet while criminals walk free. Police officers, many of whom are openly hostile towards gays, are also to be blamed for this. As a member of a human rights group, it is my belief that hate crimes, regardless of against whom, are wrong and should be condemned."

The officer noted that male prostitutes plying the streets, particularly in the resort towns of Montego Bay and Negril, are often attacked by what he referred to as "anti-gay thugs," sometimes brutally beaten to the point where they have to be confined to hospitals. He said that there is not much the police can do if charges were not brought forward. "A complaint has to be made before we can act," the officer added.

Public Defender, Howard Hamilton, said that he is outraged at the level of hate crimes going on in the country. In describing hate crimes as "disgraceful," he said that charges could be brought against people who actively seek to engage in such practices."

The Jamaican Observer
Those flamin' homosexuals

Mark Wignall
Thursday, June 17, 2004

"A little over one week ago Brian Williamson, at that time Jamaica's most vocal advocate of homosexuality, was found horrible and brutally murdered in his uptown apartment.

Based on cursory investigation, all indications are he was murdered by someone "in-house". The police report suggests that he was chopped all over his body. This is fairly consistent with previous murders in Jamaica involving male homosexuals.

While the typical heterosexual on the hunt can cruise the town freely and be socially accepted in his tomcatting, the male homosexual has to be more discreet by moving in circles where all other homosexuals also move. The real difference is, the male heterosexuals has a much larger stock of women to choose from than the smaller number of homosexuals available for the "gay" man seeking sex. For this reason, homosexuals attach themselves to each other with more rigidity in male/female relationships. If jealous rages among normal couples can be tinged with more than threats of violence in a land as violent as Jamaica, we can only imagine what it must be like among homosexuals where replacement lovers are hard to find. I am therefore not in the least surprised to read of extremely violent deaths in homosexual relationships after triangles get distorted and emotions run incongruent to passions.

Some years ago, J-FLAG (Jamaica Forum for Lesbians, All-sexuals and Gays) of which Williamson was the head, invited me to give a talk at one of their "seminars". I was contacted by a man who gave his name as Steve—just that—no surname. Over the phone I said to him, "why would you want me to give a talk at your gathering when it is obvious from my writings that I do no subscribe to you people and your lifestyle?" The voice called Steve told me that J-FLAG was seeking views for and against homosexuality.

I then asked the obvious question: Can you give me an idea of who else will be giving talks?" He told me that he didn't have the names at the time but they were well known. well, I did not go, and I have no intention of giving any talks at any one of those gatherings where those who once dwelled in the closet have not only come out now, but appear intent on forcing themselves into our collective consciousness and ultimately into our living rooms.

I see little evidence of male homosexuals being discriminated against in Jamaica. I see no evidence that our population is killing them off. In fact, what I see is probably the exact opposite: a "homocracy" in Jamaica or pockets of it where in selected circles the very best, brightest homosexuals and some not so bright are placed in high-powered jobs, in government, in the civil service, in the private sector, in the media and the entertainment industry. It seems that the Human Resource Departments of some private sector companies are willing to go the extra mile to employ homosexuals.

I have no quarrel with these workers or executives because it seems that they perform quite well. And, of course, they do not have to move too far to find a ready-made stock of people who can fulfill their sexual and other emotional desires, something, which we heterosexuals take for, granted (and abuse) at the workplace.

I agree that Jamaica's buggery laws are archaic and draconian. If two big, muscular, hairy men want to tickle each other and play pillow fight and call each other "snookums" behind closed doors, it is none of your business and it certainly is not mine. I agree that any law, which empowers the police to break down their doors and arrest them for buggery, is outdated and must be repealed.

At the same time I do not want homosexuals trying to convince my grandson that "it" is an alternative lifestyle. I don't want them writing books where a prince falls in love with another prince and they kiss and then live happily ever after. I have never burnt a book in my life, but there is a first for everything.

The American entertainment industry is overflowing with homosexuals and it has provided us with sick shows such as Queer as Folk. More than subtly, the US entertainment industry is easing homosexuality into our systems. We have to live with that.

Our local male homosexuals would like to make themselves out to be a victimized minority. Outside of a few idiotic DJs, quite a few of whom are themselves homosexuals, who are spouting there nonsense lyrics, "b******* fi dead," most of us are living with homos in our midst, and if they keep their hands and desires to themselves, we are fine.

We don't like them, but so what? They were given a bad hand at birth in this—an imperfect world. Hell, maybe they don't like us either. So what? There is space here for all of us."

mark_wignall200@yahoo.com

Interviews

I conducted interviews with over forty-five young men who are Jamaicans some residing in the United States and others currently residing in Jamaica. Some interviews were done in person while others were conducted over the phones. These are men ages ranging from sixteen to thirty-seven years old. The following questions were posed to them.

1. If a man or women raped you would you speak out about it?
2. Explain your answer
3. Do you see men who have been raped by men as homosexuals?

Responses

Edward
Age: 25
Location: Bronx, New York

"If a man were to rape me, hell I would not talk about it, I would maybe kill myself. I don't think that a woman can rape a man. A woman forcing herself on me is natural and that in my eyes is not rape. The man thing, mi no think mi could live wid mi self after all that. Honestly, I don't know if a man who get rape is gay, cause the act of homosexuality is all about penetration and yes he was. But on a serious note, no I don't think so, unless he went back for more, then he like what happen and he gay."

Oliver
Age: 18
Location: Brooklyn, New York

"Well you can't rape the willing. The idea of rape turns me on, so if a man rapes me I would go back for more, as I like it rough. My cousin raped me when I was eleven years old and then I wanted to talk, but my mother would not believe me. I don't think a woman can rape a man. As long as his penis is erect he wanted it as much as she wanted to have sex. I got rape and I turned out gay, so my answer would be yes. That is a hard question to answer, as I will use my self as reference."

Duane
Age: 37
Location: Kingston, Jamaica

"It is not practical for a woman to rape a man as there has to be an erect penis first before penetration can take place. If I were to be raped by a man, it would be hard to live with myself, as the act alone would leave me mentally unstable and I don't know if I could deal with anyone knowing that reality. I would probably kill myself and ask God for forgiveness or I would kill the man who did it to me. Reporting it would be an idea but our law enforcement in Jamaican is not trained to deal with such delicate issues and even then, I could not see myself reporting it, I would be seen less than a man. On the question of, if another man rapes a man is he gay, no I don't think so. Homosexuality is more than just a sexual act, it's a psychological make up of who the person truly is."

Kevin
Age: 27
Location: Atlanta, Georgia

"If a man raped me, then I would be a batty man and mi would kill a boy fi that. Report it, fuck no, no way on heavens could I report it. How would I look going to my family, my wife even and telling her that a man fuck me? Though it's hard to deal with, I would keep it as a secret. As a matter of fact, mi too strong fi a man hold mi down and rape me, before that happen mi kill a pussy hole. A woman can rape me any day but not a man. If a man fuck you in a you batty you a batty man."

Peter
Age: 16
Location: St. Ann's, Jamaica

"When I was younger my cousin tried to put his penis in my mouth and I told my mother and she beat me. I think it's a sick act and I would want to tell the police, but who would believe you. My family would not want me to talk, out of fear of embarrassing the family and they would keep it under quiet. I think I would run away to the US or some far country. I don't believe in suicide but I could not say in my community no more. Its the same thing if a woman had rape me, if I were to talk about it, no one would see it as rape, I would be considered gay if I saw anything wrong with it. Sexuality and the sexual act is too narrowly defined in Jamaica and too many young boys get raped and refuse to talk out of fear of being called gay. I think that more sex education needs to be thought in school. I have gay thoughts but that doesn't make me gay. If a man gets rape that don't make him gay either. To be a homosexual is when you hate women and don't find them sexually attractive no more."

Roger
Age: 18
Location: Kingston, Jamaica

"No I would not speak about it, because it is a sense of shamefulness to it. It's almost like taking off your socks and smelling in between your toes. It's something that happens to you and you just keep it to yourself. I would not know how to confide in someone telling them that you have been raped and dealing with your own inhibitions is just too much. The thought of initiating the conversation is hard. I do not consider men who have been raped by men homosexual. It's like a person who was sent to prison wrongfully would not be considered a criminal."

8

Waiting to Exhale

○ ○

"Love was always suppose to be
Something wonderful to me
To watch it grow inside yourself
To feel your heart beside itself
True love it has no hiding place
It's not something you just put away
It's always there inside of you
That's the way it feels"

—*Aretha Franklin/Baby face*

My life was going great; I was no longer at the back of my class. I moved up, my grades were better and I now asserted myself even more. As dark skinned as I am I had a glow on my face each day and all I wanted was for school to end for me to go to his house. My fear for men was no longer there as he made me feel comfortable and secure. My mother and I were still at odds, but she was never on my mind, she was history. He knew me and he was all I wanted. My bigger sister was away at college and I spent most of my time at home with my younger sister. The moment I had some free time, I would go to his house, his sister and brother knew me. I was not a part of the family but I was like a little brother. Each day after school, I would sit at his kitchen table and do my homework. Any problem I had doing the work he would help. My math and English were poor and he devised a plan to solve it. I saw being around him as being around a big brother, the brother, the man figure that I had always wanted in my life. Being at his house was like an after school program, I saw no problem in what I was doing. I knew that I was developing feelings for him and it was natural, but they were not intimate, it was more like a brotherly love.

I was proud of myself for how I was performing in school, I no longer felt depressed, hopelessly in denial of who I was. Most importantly he listened and that is what most children want, to be heard, to be respected and to be taken seriously. Many days after I was finished with my schoolwork, I would talk for hours and he would listen. I never spoke to him about my mother as while around him I wanted to block her out of my mind as much as I could. I have always enjoyed reading and I read the newspaper every day and he was impressed with that. He complimented me on my maturity and he felt comfortable talking to me about his life, his world and what he was going through. He told me about his girlfriend and that he was not yet ready to have kids but one day soon he was going to pop the question. I often avoided questions or to give any information about my childhood friend as like my mother I wanted to cut him out of my life for good. The friendship was like this for weeks, months rather and I was becoming a new man, I was confident in the way I walked and the things I did and believed in.

The new freedom my mother gave me allowed me to come in at any hour even during school nights. There were nights when she might have thought that I was in bed but I was over at his house. It wasn't as if I hated my home, I just felt more comfortable with him. We usually never talk about sex, but one day he caught my childhood playmate having sex and saw his penis and he was surprised at the size. I told him that he was small as I was much bigger and he begged to see my penis, but I could not. I never liked the idea. I felt uncomfortable. He rested the subject then, but a few days later, he repeated the request and I decided to let him see. I still felt that it was wrong. About a week later, while I was outside, talking, (we spent most of our evening chats at his gate and never inside closed doors) he brought with him a carpenter's measuring tape and he gave it to me. I had no clue what it was for, but I trusted him and thus I took it, he said measure it, I then knew what it meant and I said no need to, as it was 9inches slightly curved. He never believed me, and wanted to see, oddly enough I did have an erection but I still never wanted him to see my penis.

With all that I have been through I still never considered myself to be gay and I honestly felt that homosexuality and AIDS was a "white man" disease. If it were to ever exist in Jamaica it was the white man's fault and it was only present in the tourist areas. I never saw black men as being gay, as it was a sinful act and black people were too righteous to deal with such things. My naïve frame of mind was to be changed finally, on a dark cloudy night. After I refused to measure myself, he brought me over to his yard and I obliged to do so. His house was under construction and most of the yard was filled with mortar and sand. The sky was bright and I could see the stars, I saw the formation of the stars but could not name them, as I never took many notes in geography class. It was a damp night; I could feel the breeze on my face. He brought me into a dark corner, I was shaking and he realized and told me to relax and be calm, so I did. He knelt down before me and asked me if I knew what he was about to do, and honestly, I had no clue. He put his face close to my private area and he asked me the question again. I told him no as I had too much trust for him and never felt that he wanted to touch me in that kind of way. He touched me, I was hard, I felt scared as if he was going to hurt me, and he saw the fear in my eyes and he got up and walked away. I felt relieved, and as I walked over to him he laugh, and ask me the question again, and when he was convinced based on my facial expression. He then told me he never knew that I was so innocent.

I spent the rest of the night in his room, listening to the sound track of *Waiting to Exhale*; he had gone to Florida and had seen the movie. He collected CDs for fun and I always admired his collections. My family never owned a CD player so I would spend hours listening to his collection. He loved the sound track to Waiting to Exhale and I remember me playing number one on the sound track *Shoop Shoop* by Whitney Houston and he came over to me and kissed me. It felt uncomfortable but good at the time as this was my first kiss. I never thought much of it, but I gave an excuse about the time and I left for home. I never saw him for a couple of days, after that night but before I left his house he had given me a book to read. He told me that he saw his sister's boyfriend reading it and thought it interesting and he too felt that I would like it. The name of the book was *Just as I am* by E. Lynn Harris; this was my intellectual introduction to black gay life. I read the book and thought it interesting too but I was disgusted at the sex scene of Basil Henderson and Raymond in the pool. The thought of two men having sex was repulsive and I hated the idea.

The scene was too gross and I stopped reading the book. I was not ready to deal with what Harris was talking about and furthermore I was not interested in it. I later finished the book when I was attending University and more prepared to handle and appreciate what Mr. Harris wrote. I told him how I felt about the book and he said I was not being fair as it was not much different from what I did to his cousin, but in my mind, I was a child and these are two grown men and they should know better. Oddly enough it also turned me on, and that was a scary feeling. At that age I never knew the concept of being versatile, or being a top or bottom, but I was turned on by Basil's masculinity and I knew he was the one who was going to penetrate Raymond.

I had only a year and a half left in high school and I had major work to do before my final year. I had one major project and I failed it miserably, he was knowledgeable on the subject matter and lucky for me I was able to convince my teacher to give me a second chance and she did. He worked with me day after day and even helped me financially when my mother refused to help. If I decided not to go to school my mother never questioned why, she just asked me to give back the lunch money for that day which most times I never did. His day off from work most times was on a Thursday so I would choose a Thursday to not go to school and I would spend most of the day at his house with him. I was developing a different love for him now, as he saved my face in school, my grades and he comforted me when I just needed someone to be there.

The day I completed the project, and I was told that I got a passing grade, an A actually I was on cloud nine and right there and then I would have done anything he asked me to do and that night I was put to the test. I had spent most of the day at my mother's shop and later that night I went to his house. I was tired and I took a nap, his sister came home from work early and he said we needed to go outside, which we both did. He told me that he was proud of me and that he wanted to do something but felt that I would be uncomfortable if he asked. Seeing that he did so much for me, I felt obligated to him and I told him that anything he asked me for I will give it to him. He took my hands and walked me to a dark corner of the yard, and from where I was standing no one could see us. He went inside to see what his sister was doing and he came back with a small container of petroleum jelly. I could hear the music playing from his room, it was Mary J Blige *Not Gon' Cry*. It was damp outside as the rain had fallen earlier on that day, and I could still smell the earth with the moisture of sand and cement from the day's work as his house was still under construction.

The both of us were alone outside, standing facing each other. Mi did have an idea wa him did want, mi never did want fi do it but it was the least mi could a do, seeing the amount a help him did give to me. Mi never feel force fi do it, but something inside a mi say mi did fi do it. I needed coaching and that him did do, him touch mi up, feel mi up and say sweet things to me, just to get mi in the mood. At one point mi back was facing him and him pull mi shorts and brief down to mi ankle. Him ask mi if dat aright and mi tell him yes. Him hold on to mi waist, and him teck him time and rub him hands them all over mi body. Him use him lips and play wid mi ears and the wetness from him tongue made mi feel good all over. Mi cocky did stiff by this, cause mi did a feel some things in a mi body mi never feel before

I was about 5'8" or 5'9" and weighed about 125 lib with a slim built. Then I had no muscles, I had a frail frame, long legs, long arms, hair all over my body, flat butt, small hands, shaved head, oval face, thin lips, small nose, bright eyes shining even in the sun. I had long eyelashes, thin eyebrows and cute dimples. I had cool dark cocoa color. Even at fourteen I still had the innocence of a child, I still enjoyed cartoons before I went to school. My voice had changed but it still reflected nothing manly inside of me and I still never had a fully developed mind. I had not even fully explored my body or understood the changes puberty had left upon me and he took that all away from me.

Mi did just want it to be over, mi could a feel him behind me and all him say was to just relax cause it wont hurt. Mi try fi relax, awaiting the feel, the sensation of him, mi did fraid, and shaking as it was a bit nippy outside. Him skin did feel soft against mine; him had a light cinnamon color. Him was about 5' 7" and him weigh bout 165. Him never have no muscles, just an average guy. Him did have nuff hair pan him bady, him did have a beard, most times him keep him hear low and him face did round. Him lips were medium; him eyes them were light brown and bright, and him did have thin eyebrows. Mi could a feel him stiff buddy a beat pan mi batty. Even though mi cocky di stiff too, it never meck what him was doing right. Most fourteen-year-old bwoy get hard easy, just touch him bady and him a go get hard. The thought of sex would get mi hard, the word sex alone could. It's not so much the act but more the sensation that mi feel from a touch that would get mi hard.

Him never did touch mi wid him hands, but ah could feel him body next to mine. His buddy was pressing against mi batty. Him did a breath heavy and mi could a feel him hot breath in a mi neck back and it meck mi shiver. Ah did as I was told and him use him middle finga and him put the Vaseline around and inside of mi batty. It did painful and mi did want him fi stop. Mi never did like the burning sensation, but mi could hear him a moan and all mi did want fi do that night was to please him. In the back ground mi could a hear Chaka Khan's *My Funny Valentine* and it was as if him did a move him finga them in an out a mi batty to the slow beat of her singing. At one point mi beg him fi stop and him did stop. When mi turn round fi face him mi could a see the disappointment in a him face. Him hold mi tight and grab mi closer to him. Him wispier in a mi ears and tell mi say it would hurt the first time but him won't meck mi feel too much pain. Him say mi fi relax him point pan mi cocky and tell mi say it stiff so mi want it as much as him.

Honestly mi never did have a clue wa mi did want then, mi mind was all over the place. All mi did want fi do was to please him, him was too good to me and mi did just want fi give him something in return fi all that him did do fi me. Mi never have money so, mi did feel say anything him ask fa mi should just give it to him. Mi no know how man teck buddy but it was too painful man. Him tell mi say mi a behave like say mi a bwoy cause big man can teck buddy and no worry bout the pain. Mi never did want fi be no bwoy as him did a call mi and mi did want fi prove to him say mi a big man just like him.

Mi lack mi eyes them tight and turn mi back to him, mi did have to bend over to him lever cause him did shart and then him hold mi side and try fi put it in. All him try it just couldn't go in, mi did too tight. Him put more a di Vaseline at mi batty and with all a him strength him force him buddy inside a mi. Mi did want fi cry out, scream, cause it was as if him pap the cover off a D&G bottle. It was hurting mi, but mi did want fi prove to him say man a man. Mi did a cry but no sound never did a come out a mi mouth, then mi hear Patti Labelle singing *My Love, Sweet Love*. Mi bady did in a pain, and mi bite in a mi hand to teck way the pain from mi batty, and mi still never did want fi cry too much. This dutty bwoy, teck the one thing that mi did have left that made me a man, and him teck it way in one night.

Mi couldn't cry out loud as him sista did inside of the house and mi never did want fi cause no embarrassment pan mi self. Mi leg them did wide open and mi hand them was on the wall before me. Him never did a do it fast, but it did hurt no rass, it did a bun mi batty. Him then hold on to mi hands them and then him start to put it in futher, mi couldn't relax and the more him go inside a mi, the more it hurt mi. Mi did a try fi relax, trust mi, mi did a try but bwoy, buddy no nice. It did small to, but that is not the point, him should never did a fuck mi. Mi couldn't tell you if mi did a enjoy it or at some point it did feel good.

By the time Patti hit her last note, him cum inside a mi. Mi could a feel something hot rush up inside a mi. It was a strange feel and a sickening one at that. Mi could ah hardly move mi bady when him pull him buddy out, mi bady all over did numb, mi did want fi lick him, but him did look too happy and to an extent it made mi happy too. But fi the first time in a mi life mi did hate him. Mi never did want sex to be like this, trust me, I wanted it to be with a girl, a good looking girl, a girl with a coco cola bottle shape.

After him teck it out, him never even ask mi if mi aright, it was as if I was not in pain and him know say mi did in a pain. Mi did a wonder to myself how could someone do such a thing to a little youth. Although mi couldn't move him never touch mi at all, it was as if mi had a disease and if him touch mi him was going to get it. It wasn't even safe sex and back then, I had not much clue about STD nor HIV. Them never teach we them things a school. The night was over and him fuck mi and what else mi could a do? nothing.

The journey from his house to mine usually took me under three minutes but that night I felt like it took forever and I would never reach home. I now had regret, I felt betrayed, but who the fuck was I to talk to. I went inside my room and I was in so much pain I fell on the floor next to my bed, my butt was paining me and I started crying. I moved to go on my bed when I realized that I was bleeding and I could see spots of blood on the floor. I wanted to sit upright but I was too tender to do it. I went to the bathroom, which was next to my room. I sat on the toilet and all that came was blood and all that he had left inside of me. I tried to wipe but it hurt so f__king much, I sat whimpering. Have you ever cried before, where the tears came but no sound came from your voice? I clenched my fist, and I wanted the world to end that night, I wanted so much to scream out for help, but I was scared if I got anyone's attention, I would be blamed for allowing him to do it. The bleeding never stopped, and each time I wiped it hurt me even more and it freaked me out, this was now it, I was going to commit suicide, but I never had the strength. I had now gotten to a desperate place in my life and I wanted to end it. I never wanted to face the next day, to even look at myself in the mirror, as I felt it was my fault. But when you get to that point in your life when you want to die, but dying is so much you don't even want to live, you are at a desperate stage. I went into the kitchen and got one of the kitchen knives. I remember seeing a girl cut her wrist so I decided to do the same; I did it and the blood I saw freaked me out even more. I wanted to live but for that moment I wanted God to take the living breath out of me, and take the feeling I had at that moment away. I felt lifeless, weak, weightless, and numb. At the same point, I felt as if I was lost in deep space and if I walked or moved I was going to fall into endless space.

I decided to take a shower and I cried some more and yet there was still no sound, as I never wanted my mother to find out. What had happen. I stood in the shower, tears flowing from my eyes, my mouth was open, but no sound came out. I wanted so much to scream, to shout, and to hit something or someone. I had so much anger built up inside of me. I felt that if I had a gun next to me, I would have walked to his house and kill him. I could not deal with the embarrassment, and I could not face to tell anyone the truth about what happened. The bleeding from my butt never stopped, I sat on the toilet and even more blood came and I felt as if the living life inside of me was dead and I had nothing left to live for. I slept with a tissue tucked between my legs and I cried myself to sleep cursing God, and that night I had lost all faith in him. Why did he allow this to happen to me? As I cursed God in my mind I remember the songs playing in the background, as my friend thrust his dick in my ass.

The hardest part of waking up the next day was going to school, I never took a shower as my ass was still in pain and it hurt whenever I sat down. I knew that the day at school was going to be an uncomfortable one. There was this girl I had a crush on in my class and we had become very close friends and I wanted to talk to her but it was too hard to even tell her, as I was afraid that she was going to tell me that I wanted it. It happened, I took it and now it made me gay and the thought of being a homosexual killed me but I could not change the reality as the act was committed and I could not reverse it. I had the troubles at home to deal with and now this so I needed an escape but I saw no possible escape. I thought of going to the police, but my society is not that accepting of homosexual acts and even though I was the one that was abused I would not be seen as the victim so that was a no. I went home that day, and I packed my bag to run away but where to? I had nowhere to go. I never called him that night and I never went to church that weekend. He never called me either. A week later he called and I told him that I was still in pain and he said to stop by his house. I went. Who else was I to talk to?

I went to his house late that night and I told him how I felt about him, that I hated him and that I was still in pain. He hugged me and for the first time in one week I felt comforted. He told me that if it would make me feel any better I could do it to him. This was my one chance of getting back at him for what he did to me. He took his clothes off, put in the *Waiting to Exhale* CD, as *Shoop Shoop* started playing I remembered the night he took my innocence away from me, without asking me if I wanted to give it up so soon. My penis was much bigger than his was and being nine years younger it was all the power I had over him. He was lying on his back, his ass up. This time I was in his room, on his bed in dim lights, I could not see his face but I heard the moaning sounds he made when I inserted my fingers inside of him to get him prepared as he had done to me. I wanted to put him in pain, not only pain but I wanted most of all to rape him in just the manner in which he did to me.

I fast-forwarded the CD to Aretha Franklin *It hurts Like Hell* and I forced my penis inside of him as he had done to me, I heard him made a loud cry then he put his pillow over his face. I was rough, all I could think of was him behind me, pumping me harder and harder, I was crying but I had to get back at him. He asked me to stop and I did, because he asked me to. I wondered to myself why did he not stop, when I had asked him to. His eyes were wet and he asked me if i wanted to continue and I said yes. I fast-forward the CD to his favorite Patti Labelle. It seems as if every gay man loves her. I fucked him hard and I heard his cries but I wanted revenge. While I was tearing his ass up, I ask him why he did it and he said "if I never did, someone else would have" It was as if I gained added strength and as Patti hit her last note I pushed myself further inside of him and ejaculated. I felt cheap, filled with disgust and scorn of my own body, a feeling common among most men who have sex with men and aren't comfortable with it. I am now not sure if I had raped him, as he asked me to do it, but something inside of me said that I did. Apart from the fact that he wanted me to fuck him, he did say no, I stopped and even when he told me to continue the force I use to penetrate him was an act of rape in my mind. Did I rape Him? I put that question to you the readers. At the end of the night I questioned myself, if I had encouraged him to want to have sex with me.

As a result of my bad experience, I had a strong dislike for *Waiting to Exhale*, the sound track and the movie and I never saw the movie intentionally or listen to the CD until I was writing this chapter. It has been ten years and each time I hear any songs from the CD it makes me want to cry as it brought me back to that one night. He was upset with me because I had ejaculated inside of him and he had asked me not to. I had my revenge but it was still not enough. That night, oddly enough I felt relieved and I had a new found love for him all over again, it's a strange feeling which at my age I still can't explain but I loved him even more. He asked for forgiveness, and he told me that he never wanted to hurt me, it was just a feeling he had and he just wanted to act on it. He told me that I was his first and I believed him. He told me too that he loved me and in the weeks after that night, I found myself falling in love. I would go to school many days talking about my new love, not telling anyone that it was a guy.

We resumed having sex with each other a couple of weeks after that night, I hardly gave him the opportunity to penetrate me, but on the few occasions I did him, I would go to school the following day and tell my friends about my sexual conquest. The saddest thing about all this was that there was never a condom in place. I never thought about AIDS or HIV or that I could get it, I was so young, how could I? This was how naive I was. I wonder now, how many young boys could have gotten AIDS or HIV this way without even knowing. It's a cycle and we need to put a stop to it, all that I am trying to do is to put a face on the possible root cause to HIV and how some of our women are possibly infected. Most young boys who are molested or raped refuse to consider themselves gay, so they delve into sex with women, most times unprotected to prove their masculinity. It's a sad story but it's the reality of the world we live in.

The problems at home never changed, all my free time was spent baby-sitting my younger sister, I could never hang out with my classmates after school, and on the weekends I had my sister to tend to. I had no freedom, the only freedom I had was late nights when my mother was sleeping and I would sneak out to his house and make love to him. I wanted to tell someone what was going on, how I felt but I don't think anyone then had any idea what I was going through, and furthermore it was the only happiness I had and I refused to let it go. I had little or no trust for men or young men my age, as I was afraid that they would do the same thing that he did to me, so I had only female friends. I remember one evening after school, I sat at the front of the library crying and a classmate of mine saw me, my mother was out of the country on a visit to my grandmother and I never had to go home early. I sat outside thinking about the life I was now living and I never liked it as I wanted a girlfriend, I wanted to be a normal boy, I wanted to play soccer and I wanted to tell real stories of sex with girls. Morris saw me that day and asked me if I wanted someone to talk to, he was popular at school he sat behind me in class and often times he asked me for help and I would help him and that was it. He invited me home that day, and I was a bit scared to go with him as I was fearful of him too.

My lover had left on a business trip and my mother was still away and it was a Friday evening after school and Morris saw me once more with tears in my eyes. He invited me to his house. He lived pretty close to school so I followed him home. I told him about my problems with my mother. For the first time I saw someone show me sympathy and compassion and he told me that if I ever wanted somewhere to stay I could stay with him as his grandmother was away and he had the house to himself. That Friday evening I found a new friend and he became my best friend until he found out the truth about me and caused me my first nervous break down at twenty-two. That day he cooked curry chicken and he asked me if I wanted to watch a tape. When I answered in the affirmative he put in a porn tape of Hansel and Gretel and it freaked me out. I never wanted to show how disgusted I was at the tape as this was what young boys did when there was no adult around. We developed a special bonding that day and it changed my life. I felt young once more, I felt like a teenage boy and oh it was a great feeling. I spent less time with my lover and more time with Morris and my peers. I had gotten attached to my math and English teachers, I had developed the courage to confide in my English teacher and she offered me financial help and I was now a happy young man. Both Morris and my English teacher made my life special and they gave me hope and I thank God everyday for bringing them into my life.

I admired Morris, not in a sexual manner, but more as a brother figure. I respected him as he had a calm demur and it seemed to me as if he lived the perfect life. He played on the soccer team, which made him cool and popular among the girls, and I wanted most of all to be like him. When I watched Antoine Fisher, I could relate to his story and the friend he had next door. Morris was my friend next door. We used to talk about life, girls, school, our dreams, and our ambitions in life and many a times I wondered if he would be my friend for life. He was about 6'1", dark, long fingers, no facial hair and he had a well toned body. He was athletic so that counted for the way he looked. I would go to all of his soccer matches in support of him. His face was oval, small eyebrow, thin lips and one of the whitest and most perfect shaped teeth I have ever seen on a young man. He is intelligent, easy to talk to and most of all he has a heart of gold. The thing that I admired about him the most was that he knew when something was wrong with me even if I didn't immediately admit it and that is when you know you have a true friend. Together we would condemn homosexuality and I adopted some of his personalities and views on life. His family accepted me with open arms and for that I am most grateful. I found refuge at his house and I was happy to be accepted as a part of their family. I can still remember days on end at his house and sitting with his grandmother on the front porch. She was and still is a kind gentle caring woman who after my grandmother died gave me the love and support that a grandmother should. May God continue to bless her and give her continued health and strength.

9

No woman no Cry

○ ○
"Perhaps the biggest hurt to me is that I promised my children there would be a better life. I promised them a family. But that was never to be."

—*Winnie Mandela*

It took me years before I could confess to anyone in my family that I was molested and raped. I was ashamed of myself for allowing it to happen and I never wanted my family to face that shame with me. Something deep within me has always wanted to say something but how would they treat me, what would be their reactions? After all that have been done no one wants to talk. It is so heart wrenching that the ones you love could be so cold to you when you needed them the most. My eldest sister from my mother's side is five years older than me and as we got older we became a bit close. We have always competed with each other, more me than her. We have had our share of fights but, she was all I had, until the birth of my younger sister. At the age of twelve, my sister was the only company I had. I never trusted her while growing up, but as I got older I realized that she too had similar problems with my mother and found it hard to cope. Our relationship with our mother was one thing that kept us close over these years as we have stood by each other's side. The love that she has for me is unconditional and as I get older I realize how much she means to me.

It was the winter of 2002 and I decided to open up to someone, I was testing the family. I bought a ticket for my mother to visit me in New York and I told her that I wanted to talk to someone and I wanted her to be there. She declined claiming that she was unable to travel, so I canceled the ticket and bought one for my sister. My sister and her then husband were on vacation and she had to cut it short to visit me in New York for the weekend. The moment she arrived at JFK International Airport, she wanted to know what was up and I could see the concern in her eyes. It was painful to start I paused while pondering how to begin until she got upset and insisted that I stop playing and talk. I never minced words with her, she asked questions and I gave answers but I never called names and I never gave her too much to find out who did it either. She, like my self at one point was upset with my grandmother for not dealing with the situation but she was upset at herself for being the one who nurtured me as a child and yet she never saw any signs. She was even upset at me for not talking to her earlier and I know for some reason she blames herself for some of the pain I had gone through. We both sat and cried and we hugged each other. I had to promise not to tell my mother, as my sister felt that my mother was not emotionally ready to handle what I was going through. I knew my mother would have asked her what was going on, but I trusted my sister to keep my secret and she did.

It wasn't until 2003. The ending of autumn that I confessed to my mother about who I am and what had happened to me, and its quite obvious that she still has a lot of growing up left to do. She never took it well. She blamed me for what happened and told me that I must have encouraged it. It still hurts a whole lot, thinking that my mother blamed me for what happened. At one point during the conversation, she asked me why I did not go to the police as if they would help. She told me that I must have enjoyed it and that's why it continued to happen. As long as I live I will never forget that day, the day I came out to my mother, and the day I asked for a hug, the day I asked that we break the bridge between us. It seems that it may take death or some great sickness to bridge that gap between us. Honestly I do love my mother, but I hate her for how she has treated me over the years and how she reacted to me when I told her about the rape. To an extent it has been my mother's resentment towards me, her lack of love that has resulted in my failed relationships with women and distrust for them. I don't hate them but women can be royal bitches at times and I hope one day soon my mother will come to terms with all that she has done to hurt me.

Robin D. Stone *No Secrets No Lies—How Black Families heal from Sexual Abuse* has helped me a lot in dealing with my past and I recommend it wholeheartedly to any black family who finds it hard to accept the reality of rape within their own family. Over the years I felt that my case was unique but I now realize that it is quite common, it's just that most men don't talk about it and if they do talk, the families keep it quiet. In chapter three of her book Robin Stone deals with the family and moving beyond denial and why it is so important that victims tell their families as we can save another family member from going through what we had been though. It is also important that families who have someone who have been raped or molested, to deal with it and not keep it quiet. Silence for one can kill and the aftermath of years of silence can do more harm that good. Sure all families are dysfunctional, but that is still no excuse. Other races have dealt with such a taboo subject but as a race blacks need to fess up to their end of the bargain for the struggles of those men and women in the African Diaspora who have fought to make our lives a bit more comfortable. Education and the access to information is too easy for us as a race to sit and watch our boys and men destroy themselves. Its real, its no joke, too many of our black men are filled with anger, and this anger comes back to hurt us as a race and even harm us. Black on black crime, not only in the US is real.

I was privileged while writing this book to interview mothers and questioned how they responded to their sons when they first told them that they were raped. Most parents find it hard to accept the reality that their sons have been raped, and for others, it's more about what people think about the family and not so much what her son is going though. One Young man told me that his mother refused to accept the fact that he was raped and never wanted him to talk about it as she was a "society woman" and it would be unheard of for her son to be gay or even being rape by his father. The first step in healing as a mother is to first accept the reality of the rape, it's hard, yes I can't even imagine, but someone is hurting even more, your son. What mothers need to do is to give their sons as much love and affection as possible, blaming oneself won't solve the problem, and blaming the child will make matters worse. These are the stories of Jamaican mothers who care and have unconditional love for their sons and are hurting also.

Paulette 45 (Not real name)
St. Mary

"I cried when he told me that he was raped by the man I loved, the man who provided for me and my kids. I beat him really bad, because it had to be a lie. It wasn't until I saw the blood stain in his underwear and even then it was hard to accept the reality. I never confronted my lover, I waited seven years before I could muscle the strength to move out on my own with my other two children. By the time I had moved out my son was a grown man in his twenties. I have not said anything to him to this day as I am ashamed of myself for not believing him. I felt his pain and I hope someday he will forgive me for not believing him. It has been a great help talking to you as it has somewhat relaxed my mind. I hope that God will also forgive me for what I have done to my son, but what must I do?"

Dawn 51 (Not real name)
Kingston

"My son now resides in London, I had to run him away, case David mi man use to fuck him. Thomas was twelve when he told me what David was doing to him and I beat the hell out of him. David was a well-known gunman from R…he was not the father of any of my kids and him love pussy so a lie the boy did a tell fi get attention. Mi know say him love them cause every night him bring home food fi them. I never told David what Thomas said about him, as he would kill him. I was hardly home during the nights as mi use to sell at the dance down the road cause mi have fi survive. So most times David was home alone wid the pickney them. One night I decided to go home early as mi wasn't feeling well, mi belly did a hurt me and mi see David pan top a Thomas, mi hole mi belly and cry, mi did want fi kill him but if I did, how would I survive and take care of the pickney them? I wasn't brought up with much love, mi uncle breed mi when mi fifteen and a so mi have Thomas, so I am coming from a family of abuse. Mi never talk bout it till now. A good friend of mine use to live in London and mi beg her fi send an invitation, fi Thomas go spend summer with her and mi meck him run off. I told him why he had to stay even though he wanted to return home, but I could not allow him to be hurt no more. He is now a grown man, and he has forgiven me for what I did to him then and he is now the only man in a mi life. David died a few years after Thomas left and I was able to ask Thomas for forgiveness. He is my oldest son and mi love him but I had to do what I had to do, I never saw any other way out."

I would want to say that to be poor is a crime but I won't, these women have regrets for their actions but what they had in common was not seeing a way out of the situation. Men are somewhat more insensitive towards the issue of sexual abuse of men and it is left up to our women to deal with it. Men sometimes act irrational and violent in an attempt to resolve issues of sexual abuse. On a day when I felt I had no hope in getting help from my Country in terms of statistics, I took the chance of contacting "*The Center for Investigation of Sexual Offenses and Child Abuse*" (C.I.S.O.C.A) for the last time. I was sent pussyfooting with little or no help from Government agencies but luckily for me I came in contact with a rather interesting police officer who gave me some direction. She worked for the (C.I.S.O.C.A.) and was unable to give me the figures I required but directed me to the appropriate agency that dealt with such statistics. She was rather open-minded and asserted herself in how disgusted she was at the rate of how grown men were molesting our young boys. She assured me that men were more ashamed to report sexual abuse and young boys were afraid to speak up. In most cases she said, the abuses are often reported by a friend of the child, a teacher or a family member. Based on the information she gave me, these young men are treated with the utmost respect and their cases treated with thorough confidence.

I had asked her if at this late stage I could charge my offender, but was told that would not be possible, and she suggested only therapy could help. I was curious why the sexual offense laws do not make more reference to men being sexually molested, suggesting that sexual offense only occur against women. She also assured me that women who molest boys are treated just the same as men who molest boys or girls. Seeing that she is a part of the Government she was unable to give her personal view on whether or not the laws governing sexual abuse and their definitions were a bit outdated and needed to be revised. I asked her if she felt that if the government were to repeal the homosexual laws would it lessen cases of sexual assault of young boys by men and she was unable to give me her view on the subject. I was able to read between the lines, and I must say to the government that it is doing no social justice and "pork barrel" politics needs to end. I am making direct reference to comments made by the Jamaican Prime Minister in an article in the Jamaican Observer.

July 02, 2004, Jamaican Observer

"The British people can lobby their parliament. I am beholden to the Jamaican public and parliament."

I will strongly suggest that the government reassert itself and move beyond popular belief and do what is morally right for the good of the country and not for public popularity.

It's obvious that the Jamaican Government may not repeal the homosexual laws or revise the laws governing sexual offense, which are as medieval as our system of

Government. Might I note the Prime Ministers famous speech "I will not under my watch repel the homosexual laws". It is now left to mothers, the nurturers of society to educate their boys about sex and sexuality. It's the lack of sex education that also prevents a young boy to admit that he was molested. As care givers, women you now have a responsibility not only to yourselves but to your daughters as if you refuse to educate our young men, there will be a day when your daughters will have no one to love but themselves. Re-assess yourselves and stop defining masculinity by the standards set by our slave masters.

10

Get Up stand up

o o o o o o o o o o o o o o o o o o o o o o o o o o o o o

Emancipate yourself from mental slavery
None but ourselves can free our minds.
Have no fear for atomic energy
'Cause none a them can stop the time

—Bob Marley

As I got older, I became much wiser and I needed some place to go, not run away this time just somewhere far away to ease my mind. I was approaching the end of high school and I was eager to leave. For some odd reason being around Morris was a blessing as it was as if I had regained my youth. I now had the chance to spend more time after school and I now had a newfound interest in girls. I was still in love with Him and we made love at least three to four times a week. Something was missing, and that was the inability to share my love for him to those around me and I hated living a lie and the secrecy was killing me. I now had two best friends and they meant the world to me and I would do anything for them. School was a challenge and together we three worked it through and it was mad fun. There were days that I never saw Him and he was upset and at one point was angry at me claiming that I was falling in love with Morris, which was far from the truth. I needed Morris in my life much more than he needed me in his. He brought stability to my life and I knew for a fact that each individual that God brings into our lives, they were sent to us for a reason.

He also had a girlfriend and it seemed to me that he cared for me much more than her and in my book it counted for something. It seemed to me that he loved me and honestly enough, he was all I had, he meant the world to me, and I hated his girl, I wanted him all to myself. With all my innocence, I never cared what society thought, I knew how I felt about him and I wanted a life with him no matter what. School started to take a toll on my life, and he had gotten a new job in the city of Kingston so I saw him only on the weekends. Things never changed much, the sex was still great and he told me how much he still loved me. I remember spending one weekend at Morris' house and seeing that we had got so close, he was now my best friend and everyone knew it, I felt that he would understand what was happening in my life but I decided not to tell him about it.

When it was closer to my final exams I moved out of my mother's house, as she was really getting to me. I knew that if I had stayed in that house, I would have failed my exams as my mother placed more value on shopping (a habit that I have developed myself) rather than education. Too many nights while in the middle of studying she would call me to go do something and that pissed me off. Morris family had no problem with me being there and his family became mine and up to this day, I still call his grandmother grandma. My grandmother at the time was still my shield as she had always supported me emotionally and financially. By then my English teacher was still helping but not as much as she used to. Things were getting better, I was eating right, my grades were improving and that was all that mattered to me. I remember one day my English teacher called me after class and told me how proud she was of me and that if I worked a bit harder I would achieve ultimate success. A couple of my teachers never shared her beliefs, but look where I am now. A soft encouraging word from an adult can change a child's life forever and that day it did. If I never had a reason to sit those exams I had two, for Him and my English teacher, as they both showed me how much they cared.

While I was living at Morris' house, I use to go to his house after school and he would drop me off at Morris in the evenings. I wanted to test his love for me and I ask him if he would give up his girl for me and without even thinking hard he told me point blank NO and that hurt. His response took over my life and all I wanted to do was to fail. I wanted to escape to a far away land. It was never easy, I could not study and for the most part I could not eat, everyone saw the change in my attitude but I was too scared to tell them what was truly going on. I would talk to my friends and I would make up excuses for what was going through and blame it all on school. I regained focus on school one night when my grandmother called me to tell me how proud she was of me and that I have a chance to make the family proud and no matter what the grades were she still loved me.

That was all it took, those comforting words from grandma to make her boy pass his exams.

I did my exams and I was officially finished with high school, I was now going to clubs and I had the girls in my hand. I had one special one that most of my friends never liked but I liked her and it was sad when she told me that we could only be friends but I never felt disappointed as I had other interests and it seemed so natural. I spent the summer at Morris while my mother and my younger sister were away visiting my grandmother in New York. I was told that I could not go to New York because they had not seen my grades for the exams and only then would I get to travel to the US. By the time the summer ended and the results came, I got three A's and three B's and one C. That night I was on cloud nine and even though he had broke my heart, I still loved him and the moment I got the result slip I gave it to him to keep for a day as his work had paid off. I was beyond elated as this was now my ticket to escape, and I took full advantage of it. I was off to college for two years and it was one of the best choices I made in my young life and a period in my life I wished many times never ended.

I had to say my last good by to him and even though it was hard I had to do it. The memories of that last night are still very much strong in my head and it came back to me a few nights ago in a bar. I needed some distance from him. I just wanted to be free. It was as if he had something holding me back and I just had to go. Music has played a fundamental role in my life up to this day.

Last week, while in a bar I heard one of Whitney Houston's song and I remembered that he loved her songs, then that last night I spent with Him came back to me with a flash as if it happened yesterday.

> *"I know he is leaving me for you*
> *who said that, he told you that it was true*
> *what is he telling you, could it be*
> *Something that he told me*
> *He told me that he loved me*
> *He told me I was beautiful*
> *How did you know?*
> *Cause I played that scene before*
> *This is a repeat of my life*

> *I was his star for many nights*
> *Now the roles has changed and you're his*
> *leading lady in his life."*
> —*Whitney Houston*

It was the piano playing at the beginning of the song, it sounded so soft and gentle, the way we made love, it brought tears to my eyes and as I sat by myself in a corner of the bar I closed my eyes and cried to myself. Something deep inside of me hate Him for violating my space and confusing me even more, but somewhere in my heart I still have a place for Him as he push me a lot and allowed me to realize my dreams. That night in my room, I knew it was going to be my last and I knew I was no longer the star of his eyes as his woman was the leading person in his life.

It was a late night as always, he had company at his house and I knew how much he wanted to see me. I took the chance and told him to come over to my place. It was a full moon and I could see the reflection of the moon through my window curtain and it was like God had made this night for lovers. When he came into the room, he went straight to my bed and laid next to me in silence for quite a while. He started to question me about my plans for school and how I was going to feel leaving him.

I told him that I loved him and I don't know what I was going to do without him. He told me that no matter what happen, he would still be a part of my life, but he wanted to put more focus in the relationship with his girl. I kissed him on his lips and I meant it, he felt my passion and he held me tightly in his arms. It felt as if we were kissing forever and while we were kissing we took our clothing off slowly and laid necked in bed. I gently used my lips and made small circle around his nipples and when I had pleased my self on his erect nipples, I moved down to his navel and then to his penis. I took great care in how I held Him and how I used my mouth to satisfy him. It was as if it was my last meal and I was going to enjoy every last moment of him. I went as far as kissing his feet, something I did for the first time.

He got up and gently laid me on my back and kissed me, he could see the tears in my eyes, as the reflection of the moon was bright enough for him to see into the window of my soul. He kissed my eyes and I started to sob, as I knew this was love and I never wanted this moment to end. I never wanted to take it slow anymore as we had already taken the time to know each other. He had seduced me to the point where I was in love with him and I would give my life for him. So this time, we had to go all the way as we had already taken the time to know each other, it was our last night together and it had to be special.

I attended Knox Community College in 1996 and when I left home, I left everything behind me including Him. No one knew why I wanted to go so far away to school. Knox was situated in the hills of Jamaica far from excitement and I wanted that peace of mind for myself. I had questions to ask God and I badly needed answers, I could not accept the reality that I was gay. Knox Community College was not cheap and it wasn't that my family had money. Hell no! I just felt more comfortable going there; I wanted to start over to make my life anew. I lived off campus with five other young men and I was the youngest. My problems never changed but hey I was somewhere new, no one knew me and I could make new friends. Some of my best friends were Jay Wray and his nephews, a Jamaican brand of rum and they were all I had. It sent me to bed and when my past came back to me, I would drink and the memories would go away. I remember going to school many mornings drunk, I even did exams drunk and no one had a clue. That was what made drinking so easy, the innocent look I had, no one would suspect that I was an alcoholic. There must be a God as only he could have guided my hands on those days when I did exams in my drunken state. I never did drugs but I hung around many who did, it was fun. I had girls, yes I did, and I was now over sexed by them. It was all I needed, I thought the sex would change the past but it doesn't work like that. I also found a new sexual desire and that was oral sex, this time going down on girls.

With all the sex I was having, I never used a condom, it was new to me, and I wanted it raw. I never had sex education at home and my first introduction to sex was with a man and that was not much. I was never taught about sex in school, and the little they said it was as if sex was bad and we should never do it. If only I knew, if only my educators had done their duties and taught me what sex and sexuality was all about and not hide it from us and forced us to experiment. So many lives could have been saved and there would not have been so many unwanted pregnancies and unwanted children today. At that age in my life I never took HIV or AIDS seriously, I just never felt that I could get any of them, it was just sex. I was never introduced to STDs until my early 20s but hey, I thank God for keeping me safe and I hope to keep it that way forever.

I was young and my innocence was lost. I was now free to do as I pleased and I now had ultimate control over my life. Thanks to my boarding Miss, I was able to be myself and assert the true me. I grew to love her and had developed deep affections for her, I admired her, she was sexy, witty, fun, educated and it was all the qualities in a woman I wanted and most of all, the mother I had wanted. She was confident and stood tall, and was well grounded in what she believed in. She gave me the opportunity to express myself, to be the man I wanted to be, she pushed me, harder than anyone in my life did, even when I failed, she just encouraged me to go at it again. I learnt how to be independent and how to have faith once more and believe that if you set your mind to do something it can be accomplished. She knew I was no saint and she did warn me about my bad behavior with the girls. Oddly enough, one day after school after reading an article about the seven-year-old boy who touched my life, she told me that she would not be surprised if I turned out to be gay. I now wonder how so many people saw me being gay and I never saw it.

I now became more interested in dancehall music and artistes who I once looked down upon were like my idols. Lady Saw comes to mind, and even though she was lewd, she expressed the unheard voices of women and she was beating the odds, doing the things that men had been doing for years. She spoke up about sex, and what she as a woman wanted and it was the confidence with which she expressed herself that made me love her. "If you man lef a no your pussy fault" now that line is a classic and anytime I go to a dance and I hear any of her songs I go wild.

Apart from my new love for music, I grew in love over a period of time with a young lady. A young woman who was my ideal, someone I wanted to get married, to and have kids with and a home with a lawn. I loved her and she will always be in my heart. I remember doing everything in my powers to get her attention; I even walked her down the hill from school and followed her home on the bus. She was sexy, witty and assertive; she was a woman to be reckoned with. She was already in a relationship but I never cared. She took the time to listen to me. She wanted to know my dreams, who I was and where I wanted to be in life and no man could have asked for anything more from a woman or even a lover. We never had sex and that never mattered to me, as I knew she cared and that was all that mattered to me. The last week I spent at Knox she asked me to stay but I refused to stay, as I was sick of saying goodbyes. I gave her two of the most precious things to me and that was a stuffed polar bear that I got from my grandmother and a gold plated pen. It took me until 2003 to let go off her, as I walked with her picture in my wallet for five years just to know that everywhere I went she was close to me.

11

The real deal

"You can't just sit there and wait for people to give you that golden dream. You've got to get out there and make it happen for yourself."

—Diana Ross

I have always felt that it was the parents' responsibility to protect their child, and that was extended to the family. There is an old African proverb that says "it takes a village to raise a child" and I believe that rule up to this day and I pray that as a black community we go back to our roots and start taking care of each other. When I was first molested, I felt neglected but it never bothered me much as I really never understood what really happened. By the time I was fourteen and I was raped by my neighbor I had already learnt my social skills and my socially acceptable norms and values and yet I still never felt comfortable talking to the police. Jamaicans call the police "Babylon" which symbolizes a system of oppression and corruption. Yes, I have met a few good police in my life, my neighbor was a cop and so many times I have yearned to say something to her about what happened to me but I was scared, scared because of how the world around me would see me. When a girl is raped or molested it is seen as wrong as it happened to her because she was defenseless and weak. When the same thing happens to boys, most times they will never speak out as a society or as a race, we refuse to deal with boys on an equal level as girls. Slavery has ended but yet we still define masculinity by what our slave masters instilled in our forefathers regarding the definition of masculinity. As a society we expect our boys to be strong and brave, to be defenders of the flock, undefeated and in control.

There are laws in Jamaica that have been put in place to protect children from sexual abuse, but based on how boys are socialized they will never speak up even if anything ever happened to them, I know as I kept it a secret for close to ten years. Society has fallen short on the way in which they have socialized our boys and for that our women are paying a high price. Men and boys refuse to report sexual abuse because they don't want to be seen as weak and most importantly they don't want to be seen as a homosexual. What is so wrong in being a homosexual? We are all born with homosexual tendencies whether or not we want to accept it, yes it can be a learnt practice but so many others, based on society's view on sexuality refuse to experiment and be who they are. Having sex with a man doesn't make you a homosexual, the act is just an act. It is the mind, the mental psyche that makes you a homosexual. (opinion)

Up until I started to write this book, I thought that Jamaica did little or nothing to protect children from sexual abuse, but sure they do, I have received tons of information about the sexual abuse of young girls, but little or nothing about boys. To my surprise, the laws which currently govern sexual abuse of children, do not protect boys. Yet we wonder why our men are so angry, as no matter where we turn, no matter how bad our situation is, we are still expected to fess up, be strong and brave and take it like a man. No wonder Jamaica has such a huge gay population and they are all in hiding. In an article published in the Jamaica Gleaner, Wednesday, July 23, 2003 by Trudy Simpson, in an attempt to give credit to the Deputy Superintendent of Police (DSP) investigation of Sexual Offenses and Child abuse, still came short of the reports of boys. The article was most interesting I think, but what has happened to our boys. It was not until the end of her article she stated:

> *"The bulk of persons affected are girls but the Center is also getting reports about boys being abused."*
> *"DSP Newman was unable to break down the statistics by age group, but said children under 15 years old are also among victims in the 36 buggery cases reported between January 1 and June 30, 2003. This is up from 21 cases reported in the same period last year."*
> *"Statistics also show that there have been a number of arrests. Between January 1, and June 30, 2003, the police arrested 173 persons for carnal abuse, up from 114 the previous year; 24 persons for buggery, up from 14 in 2002 and 15 for incest, down from 29 in 2002".*

I wonder why it is, that not much resource is being put in place to allow more boys to come forward when molested or raped. I know for a fact that I never enjoyed being raped and even though the person who raped me was the one who comforted me, if I had the avenue to speak up about what had happen, maybe I could have been a better person. Thank God, I have turned out pretty good after all the hurt and abuse I have been through, but what about those young boys who don't have the support that I had or the strength, courage and determination to fight for their independence. I knew that the only way to escape all of my pain and anger was to be educated so that one day, through my life struggles I may save a life.

Based on how sexual offenses have been defined, one wonders why so many boys in Jamaica are been sexually molested and refuse to talk about it or even get help, as the main fragment of society does not even recognize the fact that it happened. It is not a poor man's crime, as yes, boys are being raped within the upper echelon of society as well as boys in the inner cities of Jamaica, because of their social standing face more burden than any other group as they have no refuge or support. While living in New York I have met upon a few who because of wealth and power were able to escape all that and they have been sent by their parents to live in the USA out of shame.

Over the years, concerns about sexual abuse have nearly always emphasized the victimization of girls and women while ignoring the reality that men and boys are also victims of sexual abuse. Sexual abuse of boys both in Jamaica and across the African Diaspora is common, underreported and unrecognized and under treated. To be identified as a sexual victim makes many boys and men question their masculinity and or sexual orientation. I still do feel ashamed at times talking about being raped and while I am somewhat comfortable talking about it, many young men and boys remain in silence. It is important as victims of sexual abuse to open up, as if the abuse is left unacknowledged and untreated, it may lead to personal and societal consequence such as depression, anxiety and other mental health problems, in addition to substance abuse, which in most cases bring about dysfunction within family structures. Most men and boys refuse to acknowledge sexual abuse, as there is this myth that suggests that all abused boys become perpetrators of abuse. This is actually a lie. Some might I add do become sexual offenders but this is not the case for most men who have been sexually abused. Those men who were sexually abused and later in life become perpetrators are in dyer need of help. Another myth is that boys sexually abused by men become homosexuals. In fact, the reality is boys who are sexually abused do grow up to be heterosexual while others become bisexual or gay. Researchers hold the view that sexual orientation is rooted in factors having little or nothing to do with sexual victimization. A child sexual orientation would have already been well established before a boy is abused. I am still not convinced on such a study, as I have no clue where my homosexual tendencies came from. While sexual abuse does not determine ones sexual orientation, what it does is to bring about confusion or feeling of negativity about their sexual orientation and their sexual function in general.

It is my opinion that not much is being done to protect our boys, not only in Jamaica, but within black communities. Out of fear, I had refused to seek help as I never wanted to be seen as weak or called a homosexual, as based on Jamaica's cultural beliefs, to be a homosexual is the most deadly of sins. It has been a most tiring task gathering information on laws governing child abuse and I was happy when I was directed to the C.I.S.O.C.A. While this group seem to have a valid objective, it is important that more be done to protect boys, and these should be clearly outlined in how sexual offenses are defined and the sentencing given to offenders. (Definitions can be seen in chapter 7) With the harsh laws now governing homosexuality, it is my opinion that men and women who sexually molest boys should have more severe penalties.

The real deal with C.I.S.O.C.A is that they were unable to give me much information in regards to incest and sexual abuse of young boys. I was able to speak with a woman who informed me that the number of cases of sexual abuse of boys are on the rise, a significant number in her opinion is still not being reported. Unfortunately there were no figures or official document to support her claim. She was however able to give me information on other organizations who may be of some help to me. Out of fear of loosing her job she said that she was limited in the amount of information she could give to me. The fact that I resided in the United States posed a huge problem as her superior were not sure what I would be doing with the information. The mere fact that I was a Jamaican and could prove my citizenship did not even count.

I was led to the rape Support Unit of Jamaica and once again they had no documentation to show the number of reported cases of male sexual abuse. A young woman however told me that "battyman" is on the rise and more cases of sexual abuse were being reported. I became quite friendly with this young woman as I was trying my best to woo her to give me some information. She was most interesting and was curious about the gay lifestyle as she felt that all gay men would molest young boys. She professed to be a Christian and could not understand why a man would want to go against the wills of God. I became furious with her when she told me that if she ever found out that her son was gay she would disown him and even have him killed. Now this is a mother, a woman who has given birth to a child, and she is also in a position to council young boys who have been sexually abuse, how absurd could she be? I had a chat with her supervisor once but it's obvious that he was a bit taken aback by the fact that I was gay, so I was at a lost.

To support my claim of sexual abuse in Jamaica I wanted more than ever to get some form of statistical information to support my claim. After weeks and weeks of being pushed around, I was able to get to Detective Inspector Barret from the statistical department of the police commoners office in Kingston. Inspect Barret from our initial conversation was reluctant to give me information. I was asked to send a fax, which I did, but was asked to resend the fax as I had used the word "sexual abuse" and "rape" in reference to men. I communicated with Inspector Barret for over six weeks. On the note of my last fax to the statistical department, Inspector Barret informed me that a man cannot be raped based on the Jamaican constitution. He argued that the rape is defined as "fear, foe or fraud inflicted on a woman by a male". He abrasively told me that a man couldn't get rape because he does not have a vagina. I was furious! I told him that I was raped, I was penetrated and sure I do not have a vagina. Inspector Barret went on further to asked me if I do not have a vagina how on Gods earth could I get rape. I told him that there is only one way a man could get rape and that is if he was penetrated from his anal area by a penis, he then told me that was not rape it was buggery.

Buggery as defined by the constitution is two men engaging in sexual acts. It is so sad that two consenting men engaging in sex could be classed with men sexually abusing young innocent boys. Now this is the real deal of Jamaica and this is the reason why men are in pain and there is nothing put in place to prevent young boys and even grown men from being sexually abused. If the laws do not protect them, who will? I was fortunate however to get my information from the statistical department of the police commissioners office. They were not of sexual abuse, they were of buggery. My source told me that in general, cases are not reported out of fear of death, the police will aid in further abusing these men as they are deemed to be homosexuals. With the system of government that deals with crimes, there is no system put in place that will provide information for male rape as based on the constitution and the cultural believes of Jamaicans, men cannot get raped. The information I was able to get gives no differentiation between buggery and male rape. The information is as follows:

Sexual Offences
For Year 1998 to 3003 & 2004

Years	Buggery	
	Rep	C/Up
1998	40	10
1999	30	23
2000	33	17
2001	29	18
2002	20	16
2003	37	30
2004	13	09
Total	202	123

Anonymous source
—Statistical Department of the Police Commissioners office, Jamaica 2004.

Extract From Crimes of hate, conspiracy of silence Torture and ill-treatment based on sexual identity

This report is one of a series of publications issued by Amnesty International as part of its worldwide campaign against torture.

The Caribbean: A colonial legacy of cruelty—Amnesty International June 2001

Although laws proscribing homosexual relations are defended in the name of local cultural values, such laws in many Caribbean countries are a legacy of the colonial past. The passionate defenses of "Bugger" laws by certain Caribbean Governments perpetuates discrimination and creates a climate conducive to violence against lesbian and gay people, both at the hands of state officials and of others in the community. In a submission to the UN Human Rights Committee on Trinidad and Tobago in October 2000, AI stated that the retention of laws, which treat homosexuals as criminals, lends support to a climate of prejudice, which increases the risk of attacks, and other abuses against people believed to be gay or lesbian. Reports suggest that such laws are often used by the police to extort money from members of the gay community.

Four men were arrested near the airport in Kingston, Jamaica, in November 1996 and charged with "gross indecency". The men, two of whom were partially clothed, were forced to remove all their clothes and held naked in public view at the airport police post until the following day. An angry mob gathered, allegedly in response to incitement by police officers, and threatened the men. The four were then driven to the Rape Unit where they were allegedly sexually assaulted before being transferred to the Remand Center where they were forced to clean inmates' cells and toilets with their bare hands. Police also incited other inmates to assault the men and left their cells unlocked so that other inmates could enter and beat them.

This is one of a large number of reports received by AI of ill-treatment of gay people in Jamaica. Most reports are anecdotal or anonymous, usually because individuals fear reprisals if they complain. Consensual sex between men remains punishable by up to 10 years; imprisonment with hard labour.27 Such laws appear to be seen by the law enforcement officials as a license to ill-treat people believed to be homosexual. They also encourage physical attacks against gay people in the boarder community.

Released prisoner rapes 12-year-old boy, charged with buggery

Observer Reporter
Monday, March 14, 2005

JANET fears for the sanity of her 12-year-old son. He only sits and stares off into space, traumatised from being raped in his community by a man recently released from prison. The rape, says his mother, was brutal, leaving physical injury. "He was raped badly," she said.

The alleged rapist Roy Blackwood, said to be in his early 20s, was arrested Tuesday for the crime. It is also alleged by the community that Blackwood had earlier attempted to rape another boy in the rural St Elizabeth community and his own younger brother.

The community, upset that they had not got the chance to beat Blackwood, advised the Observer of the rape. They were upset that the police had whisked him from the area without their knowledge.
The police at New Market say Blackwood has been charged with buggery, but were unable to say immediately when he would face the court.

On Thursday, sounding confused, frightened, angry and in pain, Janet - whose surname and address the Observer is withholding so as not to identify her son - wondered at the callousness with which her child is being treated. The police came, she said, to take statements, but refused to treat her son "as a person."

The investigator, she said, refused to look at the boy, and having advised Janet that he had to take her son to the hospital for an examination, decided he was too busy and called another colleague, a female, to get it done.

At the hospital, despite her insistence, Janet was barred from the room where her son was taken to be examined, with the off-hand comment: 'Is police business dis.'
He was examined, but the doctor did not treat him, said Janet.
"Not even little medicine dem no give him," said the distraught mother. "Suppose him have AIDS. Nothing dem no tell me."

But he did get a brown envelope, with what Janet believes might be instructions but which she did not understand.
Her only hope at the moment is that the Victim Support Unit (VSU) can help her figure it out.

"Dem call and say me must come with (my son)," she said. She was to have gone Thursday morning, but having paid for medical treatment, Janet had no money to pay for transport into Santa Cruz where the local VSU is located, she said.

12

I Don't Wanna Cry

What is life?

What is life when there is no breath to breathe?
What is life when your inner soul is lost?
What is life when all hope is lost
And you have no where to turn?
You sit by yourself, listing to your heart
To give a pounding beat.
Where is my life?
Often at times I am alone
Wanting to be loved by someone.
I wonder what life is.
—O'Brien Dennis

Between 1996-1997 I went through a series of mental breakdowns, I wanted to die I was questioning God more and asking him "why me?". The sexual abuse and the love I had lost was taking a toll on me, I wanted to reach out to someone but I was scared that if I tried once more, the same thing would happen to me again. I was constantly depressed, lonely, and scared of living. I wanted to die, but I was even scared of doing that also. 1996 was filled with sex, and alcohol, but what 1997 was to bring to me I was not prepared to deal with it. I remember watching this program on TV about a young girl that was raped and she was scared to talk about it, and the doctor told her, if she could not find the words to express how she was feeling she should write them down. I started to keep a journal, my journal became my best friend, whenever I felt lonely, and I would sit down and pour my heart out in writing. It felt good, as the book was my best friend I could write anything hoping that no one would find out. The sex continued and sure, my other best friend was liquor, how could I ever give up my first and only best friend, it was not easy, but later on in life I realized that some things we ought to let go of as it can destroy us. Many men and boys drink, to get rid of the pain, I do understand but never let the liquor get the best of you, the best help you can give yourself is to first acknowledge that the abuse occurred and the next best help is to talk about it. Nothing is wrong with crying, crying does not make you less of a man, for me, I find more strength in crying rather than using that built-up anger to do something that may cause me more pain.

1997 is still one of my most painful years to this day. The one man whom I admired and who inspired my political ideologies, tact and diplomacy had died. He was the late Michael Manley (then Prime Minister of Jamaica). It was also the year that Britain had lost the peoples' Princess. I recorded these pain stricken days, and reading them now is like therapy. Sometimes in order to let go of our past we have to re-live them and as I turn the pages of time, I realize how much I have grown; it has taught me how to forgive. Just as how God has forgiven us, he also expects us to do the same.

Sunday, August 31, 1997

"Great Britain woke to the tragic news of the death of her Princess, Diana. She could be described as a colossus, a beautiful charming young woman who has taught the world how to love. She cared for everyone, and this was evident even in her numerous amount of charities. Her memory will live on forever."

It was also the year that mother Teresa. The Nun, who through compassion and love dedicated her life to save the World died. It was also the year that God took away from me the only comfort I had in the world, the one person who loved me unconditionally, my Grandmother. It is now seven years since her passing and it feels as though it was just yesterday, I have not mourned her death and I sometimes wonder if I should. It hurts to know that she has gone but her memory still lives on inside of me.

Thursday, July 10, 1997

"Grandma died today. I was warned from early in the morning that she would not live. I heard about the quarrel, I was so darn upset I could not move a muscle. I was expecting anything. It was late evening when she died; I am now life less and have nothing else to live for. My thoughts are shattered and the more I think about her, the more my body aches. I want to cry but no matter how hard I try the tears won't come out. One should never question God, but why did you take her so soon. She died with her pride and dignity, and it was so good that she never had to suffer."

I still have the last note she gave me, in the back of my journal. I had gone to the Cayman Islands on vacation and she never wanted me to go and I felt that she was upset with me, but her love was unconditional.

"Son"

You make me and the family proud, but the most important person in life is you. So far is son, the sky is the limit. With all the best thing that the world has to offer you.

Love

Grandma

The days after her death, I had a never-ending pain all over my body. I could not cry, my body felt lifeless and I just wanted to fall asleep and not wake up. Whenever I am hurt now, I close my eyes and imagine myself on a high mountain and picture myself jumping but the reality of my fantasy is that there is no were to fall. I no longer had any recollection of my past. I was angry with God. With all the pain that I was going through my family never had a clue about the pain I was going though; I was taking it all like a man, not showing any emotions, I was just a boy trapped in the mind of a man. The immediate family was all consumed with what Grandma had left behind and who should get what. I just wanted to talk to someone. It was the summer Biggie Small died, and it was the tribute song Faith and Puffy sang that comforted me. In the shadow of all the pain I was going through, my only refuge was the liquor, I marvel how no one ever saw, but I was a man and no one took notice of what I was doing.

Saturday, October 11, 1997

"I have lived a life filled with dreams, just like any ordinary teenage boy, my needs are just the same. I never really had much of a childhood as such, playing and having a life filled with fun and laughter. I was forced to deal with the struggles of life and wanting everything that was out there. Failure was never yet apart of me. The things that power and influence can do are numerous. At one point in my life I was troubled, lonely, some times I hate talking about it as it was like a nightmare which has haunted me every day of my life, which allowed me to constantly blame myself and continue in that trend believing that it was natural."

Saturday, October 25, 1997

"To a point he wasn't so straight and I really wanted to understand. My lover, he was the fucking one. Well I asked him the question, which I have always wanted to ask. He was very much angry and wanted to get a definite reason why the question was asked, but I could not honestly give a reason. Unfortunately I was able to bring the question to a lower level. Why did you take my innocence away?"

October 31, 1997

"We sometimes feel lonely and empty inside, but all that matters are true friends and companionship. I want someone but why should I bother myself with it or even worry about it too much. True friends is all that count."

November 9, 1997

"I am unable to recall the following events in my life, my soul is now left empty and my life shattered like drops of blood after a gruesome murder. My body is now aching for love and comfort; my hands are coerced like desert sand my limbs shiver as if I have lost my zeal. My prick for one no longer has any direction, just hope it does not turn back as it my cost me my life."

Monday, November 10, 1997

"I vividly remember that I wrote an interesting poem in high school. My pussy is big, my pussy is black, when I am glad it is sad. It was only last night when I started to play with the head of my c____k. Its length has always amazed me. The vanes are huge, it feels as if the blood had left my brain leaving me unconscious."

Sunday, November 16, 1997

"Today was the creation of history. It was the final qualifying match for Jamaica to qualify for the 1998 World Cup. Ms, _____ was not home, that's number one Unfortunately, Jamaica drew the match and qualified for France."

Sunday, November 23, 1997

"Today was a very bleakly day, it kind of made me feel down. I bought the weekend paper and read my literature book. I slept for a long time after so that I could be able to study later. To tell the truth, I now see myself confused, depressed and lifeless. What has my life really become? School is gradually becoming a drag. Where am I going?"

Wednesday, December 10, 1997

"Today is my sisters' birthday and I am unable to fulfill my promise to her, eventually I bought her the gift. I did something today that could destroy my friendship with a good friend; I had phone sex with his girlfriend. She came four f___king times, I jerk off but never came, I wanted someone so badly. I decided to skip classes today to go to the river, it was the one place I felt a peace with myself. I remember many a days contemplating jumping from the cliff were the water was cascading from the falls. I yearned for death but just never knew how to do it?"

Sunday, December 14, 1997

"It is close to the holidays and school will be out soon. I hated the idea of going home as it would brought me back to that night and I wanted to block it out of my mind so much. My mother finally called; at least she is finally showing some interest in my life, I hope that it continues. There is a pain in going home and leaving my friends all behind. School has given me the refuge to hide and not deal with me. I got drunk last night but who cared, no one cares about me."

The diary entries above represented the period in my life when I attempted to commit suicide. Of the three times I tried to hang myself the rope could not knot on one occasion and on the two other, it was not strong enough. I had wanted so much then to die, the more I consumed myself with the liquor, the more I felt like dying. By the time I had completed my last year in college it was alleged that I had gotten a girl pregnant, I never tried to find out if it was true as I had no interest in another life, I didn't even want mine.

I made a promise to God, that if he guided me though all that was going on in my life and if he made me pass my exams to go to University, I would make a conscious decision to change my life. I knew for a fact that if I never passed those exams, that would be it for me, death was inevitable. I have now come to understand God's love and his love is unconditional. Everything that happen in our life happens for a reason, it is just for us to take the positive out of it all and make some good out of it. It is hard at times to understand the things that we go through, but God has a plan for each and every one of us. Because of God's undying mercies, he saved my life, to be an inspiration to others, I now have no regrets of the things that happened to me in my past, there were worst to come, but I was able to better understand them. In all the things that I do, I put God first, he taught me faith and how to live again, he taught me how to love and most importantly how to love me first. My definition of love comes from the bible.

1 Corinthians 13: 4-8

4. Love suffers long and is kind; love does not envy; love does not parade itself, is not puffed up;
5. Does not behave rudely, does not seek its own, is not provoked, think no evil;
6 Does not rejoice in iniquity, but rejoices in the truth;
7. Bears all things, believes all things, hopes all things, endures all things.
8. Love never fails. But whether there are prophecies, they will fail…

Sex is not love, neither is money, wealth or fame. I have the gift of life. I made a promise to God to seek help, to understand the past and even though it was hard, I had new challenges ahead of me and it was imperative that I sought help. I wanted so much then to know who I am and my purpose in life and today my life has touched so many people, I now want to continue to live a bit longer. The struggles never end but I eventually found my place in life. I have now realized that my happiness is my choice and only I alone can make me happy. I must first love myself before I can love others.

Part II
Changes

13

Truth Hurts

o o o o o o o o o o o o o o o o o o o o o o o o o o o o o o

"Another time, another space
Mark my words I can't fake another day of stress
My hearts been taken whole
and this dream is getting old…
Woman, feeling good about the choice I made
In so deep there aint no judgment day
If there was, I think I'd be okay…
Woman, please release me from your hold tonight".

—*Remmy Shand*

For some of the women whom I have been with throughout my life, and who will read this book, to them it will be more of a confession. I have lived a doubled life and I have kept secrets from these women, not because I wanted to, but because I had no choice but to. I never meant to hurt any of them, I was trying to be the man I was taught to be, strong and independent and not show emotions. I never wanted to lie, but I feared most of all in losing them. If I had my life to live over again, I would have been up front but its now in the past and now this is the present and this is the truth. There is one woman (Kisha) who I pray each day was still in my life and I hope each day that she will find a man who will love her for her, as she had given me the ultimate respect and space any man could desire. I loved her then and I love her now even more. She knew that I was hiding something, but she was caring and she gave me room to be comfortable enough, hoping that I would be open to her, but I never did, and when I did it was too late. I am sorry, I tried, but honestly it was never easy, even now it still isn't. I was quick to conform to the roles society put me in, I knew what society expected of me and I played into it. I played into my relationships, as I felt forced to be with these women.

I don't know if being molested or raped has caused some men to become gay or bisexual, but I do know one thing for sure, and that is I am not with a man for sex. The thing that made Kisha special from the rest was that, she never forced me into a societal role. She gave me that emotional connection that I now desire from men. Intimacy is not all about sex, its about the hug, the cuddle and the warm embrace that someone gives to another, some women don't know how to be intimate as they were taught it seems, to please only from within their legs. If that was all, I would be overly pleased. I honestly think that women are too caught up with the role society prescribe for men. There are times when a man wants to be led, to be pampered, to be nurtured, and to be loved, it sometimes takes just a listening ear, men too have problems, and if we cannot talk to the ones we love we will go elsewhere. Sometimes I would want to cry and pour my heart out, get rid of the pain I have stored inside of me all these years, but I was scared of being seen as weak. There were days I wish I could find a woman who would not be selfish and listen to my problems too, no wonder gay men and lesbians are so popular as one of the things they do and that is listen.

Not all men who are molested or raped turn out to be gay or even bisexual, the act alone as I have noted earlier does not make you gay. With the anger and pain men who have been raped or molested have to go through, most times they live a double life or on the down low (DL). The sexual stimulation of the rape or molestation occurred so often it became a part of their lives and it is so hard to let go of it, so as they become adults they continue to engage in these sexual acts with men. Its not easy to understand how the one thing that has caused so much pain, can actually force you to want to continue but, its common sense, if you do something continuously, it becomes a part of you. Men often times hate the thought of living a double life. There is something inside of them that cannot let go of the past, the feel, the sensation of being raped or molested. It's hard to let go of the first sexual touch. The DL phrase has now lured itself into contemporary society, these are men who sleep with men on the "low" and yet they don't associate themselves with the gay lifestyle. Some men on the DL do it not for just the sex, it's more the emotional bonding that comes with being with a man, thus its more mental than physical. J.L. King in his book *On the Down Low: A journey into the lives of "Straight" black Men who sleep with me,* gives a fitting explanation of why men sleep with men. I have read his book twice and women, I think you should take the time to read it for yourselves, as it will open your eyes a bit more. Men, you too should read it as some of you need to be more manly and be honest about who you really are.

King talks about dominance and this is one of the main reasons why some men rape and molest young boys, to be in control. The only way to stop the cycle is to deal with the issue, come to terms with the fact that it was not your fault. I am not saying to parents that they should suspect all young men who hang around their sons, but if your child's attitude changes over night, check it out. Talk to your son, give him that freedom to be himself, to get in tuned to his emotions and comfortable with his body, so if he is violated in any way he will be comfortable to speak up. The same way you teach your female child to talk if she is touched in that private area teach your boys also. Mothers need to stop teaching their young boys to be rough, tough and mean, most times you say you want a man to understand you and be more in tuned with your emotions, but when you all teach your boys to show no emotions what do you expect?

I must note that not only young boys get raped; grown men do get raped also. I have realized that grown men find it even harder to deal with rape than young boys; it strips them of everything, not only their masculinity but their sanity. These grown men are more prone to commit suicide and be physically abusive to their women. That anger that is within them can turn to an evil monster and create havoc on society. During the prison riots in Jamaica of 1997 one white-collar prisoner spoke out candidly about being raped in prison repeatedly by the prison warden. He is married with two kids and does not consider himself to be gay nor bisexual. He was convicted of a white-collar crime and put among hardened criminals to do hard time.

He argued that he knew homosexuality existed within the prisons but initially he was never approached or forced into any sexual acts even though so many were forced into doing it. It wasn't until three months in prison that he was forced to have sex with the Prison warden. He explained that the warden told him that he protected him for all this time and for being so kind to him and it was now time to pay up. The warden asked him if he knew that he had a slim body and a cute face and no one touched him, and that was because he ensured that no one did. He explained that for the first couple of weeks he would bleed repeatedly and found the pain unbearable. He said he fought each time he was forced to do it, and the more he fought the more it hurt. He said he eventually relaxed as he knew no matter what he did, the guards were still going to hold him down and allow the warden to f..k him. He explained that the pain he felt turned into pleasure and that each time he yearned to be penetrated. He is now out of prison and even though he does not associate himself with the homosexual life, he said he occasionally picks up boys in New Kingston just for sex. He claims that he never allow anyone to penetrate him as it brought back too many memories of his prison life but he found pleasures in inflicting pain on young boys, who are vulnerable and easier to attract because they need money.

I must point out that during his prison ordeal, a condom was never used, lucky for him he never got an STD or HIV but there are many men who have similar stories like him who get a sexually transmitted disease. These men when released from prison sometimes are infected with the HIV virus, return to their girlfriends or wives and continue sex. Even though many have participated in sexual acts among men, they do not relate to the gay life and some do not practice those acts beyond the prison gates. The sad story in all this is that too many women are infected by these men. HIV is on the rise in Jamaica among women and not only in Jamaica but it's a universal trend. The effects of rape and molestation of young boys has a ripple effect and has numerous implications, which is destroying the black community, not only Jamaica. Jamaica is only an example of the general attitude of blacks about sexuality, incest and rape.

Jamaica Aids Support

4 Upper Musgrave Ave
Kingston 10, Jamaica
(876) 978-2345

Female HIV infection rising

Wednesday, June 30, 2004

"The number of women becoming infected with HIV is fast catching up with the number of men, research has found.

Healthcare analyst Research found that this was mainly due to the fact that 51% of newly diagnosed HIV patients contracted the virus through heterosexual contact compared with just 36% through homosexual contact.

Ten years ago, the split was 28% heterosexual against 38% homosexual.

The rest of cases contracted HIV through non-sexual contact.

Experts are warning that this shift towards heterosexual infection carries with it the risk that increasing numbers of babies will be born to HIV positive mothers.

And it raises questions about which HIV treatments can be safety used during pregnancy.
But at present, ATZ is the only drugs fully approved for use during pregnancy.

The researches focused on 3,000 patient across Europe who were being treated for HIV infection between July and October 2002.

Complacency

Researchers Amanda Zeffman said the figures suggested a worrying level complacency about HIV among the heterosexual community.

She said: "Government must now turn their attention to the rise in transmission via heterosexual contact.

Ministry of Health
Health Promotion & Protection Division
Oceana Building, 4th Floor, 2 Kings Street
Kingston Jamaica West Indies
Tel: (876) 967-1100-1

National HIV/STD Prevention & Control Program
Acts and Figures
HIV/AIDS Epidemic update 2004

The rate of HIV infection in Jamaica showed a marginal increase of 8.2% in 2003 compared to 2002.

The rate of HIV infection in women is increasing steadily more than men.

January-December 2003, there were 67 children under the age of ten years newly reported with AIDS compared to 81 children in the previous year.

The decrease in the number of reported children with AIDS indicates the improved services in the prevention of mother to child transmission of HIV program. There has been fewer pediatrics AIDS deaths (29 cases) compared to 45 in the previous year. This is also attributed to the improvement in care and treatment for HIV infected children and decrease in MTCT.

For every thousand pregnant women in Jamaica sixteen are infected with HIV. Higher rates were still reported from western parts of the island, St. James.

Adolescent females in the age group 10-19 years had twice and half times higher risk of HIV infection respectively than boys of the same age group. This is as a result of social factors where by young girls are having sex with HIV infected older men.

HIV/AIDS and Sexually Transmitted Infections are the second leading cause of death for both men and women in the age group 30-34 years in Jamaica.

An estimated 120 or more children under the age of 18 years were orphaned by the loss of one or both parents in Jamaica, 2003.

In 2003 every week 12-13 persons died of AIDS in Jamaica.

The average length of hospital stay for an HIV infected or AIDS patient is 12 days. Seven hundred and seventy on (771) persons with HIV/AIDS were admitted to hospitals in 2002.

National HIV/STD Prevention & Control Program
Facts and Figures

Thirty five percent (35%) of all reported HIV/AIDS cases in Jamaica are in the age group of 30-39 years and 20% of all cases are in the age group of 20-29 years.

St. James and Kingston & St. Andrew recorded the highest cases of HIV/AIDS in Jamaica. However, parishes such as St. Catherine, St. Ann, Hanover showed a very rapid increase in the last year compared to the previous year.

One out of five persons with tuberculosis infection had also HIV infection.
33% increase in the reported AIDS cases was registered in persons over the age of 60 years.

Summary of information can be found at the Jamaica Ministry of Health website: www.moh.gov.jm

I have often asked myself if women are prepared to deal with the reality of life. Grown men who are survivors of rape or who have been raped in their adult stage refuse to speak openly of the abuse, not because they are scared but more out of the fear of resentment by women. Women can be horrible beasts and when they turn their backs on a man they turn their backs. It's hard when you have spent years building on a relationship and something horrible happens and out of fear you remain quiet. Many men want to speak up, but women will you listen, feel their pain and burn those bridges? A friend of mine said that he refuse to tell his wife about his past because he doesn't want to bore her with his troubles, life was going too great for them for him to do that to her. The question really is, how can he do that to himself? It takes courage and honesty to be open not only to yourself but to others. I have come clean with all my girlfriends about my past and each time I talk about it I am continuing the healing process. Life is like an old country road at times with no nothing but a long stretch of road, but at some point of the journey there is a bridge to cross, so men tough up and walk over it, save a life, your own.

14

Street Boys

○ ○

"The Street boys are not really gay, but the uptown men in their big SUVs target me.
Once one held me up in the Molynes area with a gun, demanding oral sex".

—*Devon (not his real name)*

There is a direct correlation between sexual abuse of boys and street boys in Jamaica. I am not suggesting that all street boys are sexually molested but in most cases they are left in the open and vulnerable to be molested by grown men. According to the National Institute for Street Children (Jamaica), there are three types of street children; homeless children, children who go home now and then and there are children who hustle on the streets and go home. According to the Hon. Olivia "Babsy" Grange, (member of Jamaican Government) the number of street boys is estimated at 10,000! The increase in street boys has escalated over the past 10-15 years. In a United Nations report, entitled *Profiting from Abuse" An investigation into the Sexual Exploitation of Children,* states that a study shows that boys at higher risk tend to be under the age of 13 years old, non-white, of low socio-economic background and not living with a father or male figure. The report found that in Jamaica, 13% of 450 school children in Kingston aged 13, 14, and 15 years, have reported the traumatic experience of attempted rape. It is important to re-emphasize that sexual abuse of boys are still under-reported, under treated according to the UN report. Before I discuss the relationship between sexual abuse, child prostitution, the spread of STD and street boys, I will first paint a picture in the minds of the readers of the life of street boys in Jamaica.

'*My father threw me out when I was 19 and threatened to kill me*'
—*Ann Margaret Lim*
Sunday, November 09, 2003
The Jamaica Observer

"Devon never chose to 'hang out' on street corners in his boyhood. Instead, he studied hard and passed his Common Entrance Examinations, earning a place at Ardenne High School.
He was determined, he says, to complete his secondary education, despite the difficulties he experienced because of the constant conflicts he had with his parents, mainly his father. "My father threw me out at 19 and threatened to kill me," Devon tell the Sunday Observer.

Today, Devon roams the streets of upper St. Andrew—alone.

"The street youth's dem dangerous against each other, as dem same one want to kill yu or just use yu," Devon says defending his lonely silence.

The handsome 25-year-old says that while he lived at home, he had numerous girlfriends who all left him because of his father's allegation that he is crazy and on drugs.

Devon speaks relatively good English, when not conversing in the dialect. In fact, his grammar is a tad better than, Michael's, Peter's and Andrew's, but his eyes are just as sad as Michael's—possibly sadder. At no time do they reflect the slight level of comfort as those of the other three. In fact, Devon appears tortured and extremely unhappy.

According to Devon, things got progressively worse between himself and his father when his mother migrated to Canada. He is convinced that his father tells his mother lies about his whereabouts when she calls. As he describes the tumultuous relationship between himself, his father and stepmother, the troubled young man vows never to return home. "I went there about three months ago, but they found a way to kick me out again, after two weeks," he says. "Although the police came and told my father that I am his son and things should be worked out, he has to please his wife. Even whilst I was there, they didn't feed me and I was mainly outside."

The slightly chiseled young man, who says that he was robbed shortly after he went to live on the streets, is no longer a target for thieves, as he now walks barefooted and has minimal clothing. "What they want from me now is sex," he explains. "The street boys are not really gay, but the uptown men in their big SUVs target me. Once one held me up in the Molynes area with a gun, demanding oral sex. I only got out of it because I tricked him and told him to take off his pants. While he was doing this, I ran," says Devon.

His typical day begins at 6:00 in the morning when he rises from his 'bed' in an open lot on Constant Spring Road and sets about getting money from begging and running errands for people.

STREET BOYS, street wise—My Life as a street boy Jamaica Gleaner

Merrick Andrews, Staff Reporter
Saturday, August 11, 2001

"YUH a nuh big, strong bwoy? Gwaan go look work, "answered well known DJ Buju Banton when I begged him for money recently. The entertainer and his crew looked me up and down.

I was dressed in a faded pair of crumpled and dirty-looking jeans, black shoes cracked with age, and a cap turned backwards on my head.

Although I was only on assignment to find out what it was like being a street boy—albeit for only part of a day—I felt ashamed.
Hands in my pocket, I walked off slowly as the light turned green—humiliation rang in my ears as they drove off.

As "a hungry and poor street boy, 'I had expected generosity from the DJ whose songs express sympathy for ghetto youth.

After two hours on the streets—the stoplight at Marcus Garvey Drive (across from the Tinson Pen Aerodrome) in Kingston—it's easy to start feeling like a piece of useless junk.

FAMILY 'JUGGLING'

I also came to realize that the street boys I encountered worked like a family. Dazzie for example, the boy who encouraged me to Ask Buju Banton for money, was angry at the way I was treated. "Mi nuh ask dem bwoy di fi money," he said, as if to assuage my hurt feelings.

....

Eventually I crossed to the other side of the street where five older-looking boys were busy plying their trade. They bombarded me with questions, wanting to know how I would get my next meal, where I lived, with whom and whether I attended school. They also suggested that I apply for a job at the nearby wharf because I looked like a "bright bwoy"

"So why yu guys nuh get a job?" I asked. They told me that they had no education, had been on the streets since they were toddlers and preferred to 'juggle' than work for someone else.

Like Dazzie, they wanted to ensure that I earned some money but, commenting that I looked "desperate" they gave me $70—mainly in coins—and cornbread."

These boys are savvy, street smart and intelligent. They are caring loving boys who like any other boys their age have dreams and hopes of a brighter future. The only sad thing is their circumstances; they have been given a raw deal in life. All these young men require is love and someone to show them that they care and a chance at a better life. I have always wondered why we ignore our street boys. They are so visible, yet limited resources are spent to protect them and the church turns a blind eye to them all. Jamaica is a class-structured society and the Church propagates this class division and these boys aren't worthy of help.

While these young men struggle to survive by begging, at times they meet up on professional men who are willing to help them. They may not give them a home, but some encourage them to go to school, some even pay for their schooling and ensures that they have a healthy meal. Some of these men do this out of the goodness of their hearts while others ask for sex in return for their kindness. For most of these boys its hard to choose, so they give these men sex and sadly enough they don't consider it rape, and they sure don't associate themselves with the homosexual life. No matter how it is looked at, these boys are being taken advantage of and they are sometimes forced into prostitution.

The street boys of Kingston, Montego Bay or any popular tourist town across Jamaica are similar to most cities around the world. When day turns to night, street boys turn to the streets and sell themselves. On my last visit to Jamaica in 2002 I spent a night with a friend of mine on the streets of New Kingston observing these young boys sell themselves. It is reported that they get more sales than female prostitutes. I observed a grown man, in his late forties approach this young boy no older than 16 and lured him into his BMW. 45mins later he dropped the boy across the street from the Hilton Hotel. My friend and I approached the young boy, implying that we desired his service; he gladly obliged and came into our car. I questioned him about his trade and how he was paid. He received about $500-$1,000 for any form of sexual favors. He argues that he wants to stop but he has no home and his mother doesn't have enough space at home for him as there are twelve of them in all. He argues that each time he has sex with men, he feels a sense of guilt and shame but he takes the money home to his mother to support his brother and sisters so he feels he has no choice but to continue.

Dwight is the name of the young man we spoke to and he told us about the warts and bums he has at his ass and wants to go to the doctor but is scared. He says even though his bruise and cuts are visible, men still insist on sleeping with him. He argues that most of the men he sleeps with are doctors and lawyers and he has even slept with a politician once. I gave him $50.00 US not because I had it, but my heart went out to him and I wished I could do something to help or even tell him that there is hope beyond the streets.

Older street boys not only rob younger boys but they also use them for sex. One boy I spoke with told me that he is not gay but since that he lives on the streets and wears shabby clothes no girl will want him, so what else should he do. Even though both men are young it is still sexual abuse as the younger one does not want to engage in sex. There are even older men who are not homeless who sell these boys in return for cash. They are like big brothers and they give them money and protection in return for them to have sex with men. This sort of activity is more structured and organized than anyone could imagine. Because homosexuality is illegal in Jamaica it is difficult to find a male partner so men solicit the service of these young boys. Poor men don't buy sex, as it is easier to lure a poor boy in his community to engage in sex with him. The elitist group within the Jamaica society solicits these boys. I don't know the names of any men of affluence who have solicited street boys as these boys are bound to secrecy thus the reason the trade thrive undetected.

We can look beyond street boys and we will realize that other boys within the Jamaican society are lured into the arms of men, not just poor boys, but boys who are involved in sports and any organized activities. Sexual abuse of boys exist within every fabric of Jamaican society, it's just that Jamaica is a country that lives in constant denial about its existence. Sexual molestation of boys does not only happen within all male schools it exists in Co-Educational schools as well. A few of my friends who attended a popular all-male school, strongly deny that boys are molested, but it's a fraternity of men and they are all pledged to secrecy. Boys are molested at camps, be it church or school camps, but often times they usually never speak up. Young boys are also sexually molested within organized sporting activities, not only by their coach but also other members of the team.

I am not an avid sports fan, but I enjoy the game of soccer, I can't play well, but I will try my skills at the game if I find good company. Sports are considered a man's game, and everything about it is considered manly. Jamaicans love sports, it's obvious in the way the country idolized the "Reggie Boys" at the World Cup in France. Soccer practice at times is more than just practice, it's where men do men thing and sexual acts among men is sometimes considered a right of passage in some sports. I remember watching the Manning Cup in high school and saw the boys playing in their shorts wet from perspiration and I could see the imprint of their penis, damm!! it incited something in me. I wonder if any touching goes on after practice. I now know of guys who I went to school with who played on the football team who were popular with the girls and I can assure you that they are gay. I was taken aback by an article I read in the Jamaican Gleaner shortly after I left Jamaica. It was about a young man who used to play for a prominent high school in Kingston on the Manning Cup team and he was involved in a relationship with a supporter. He was seventeen when it all started. I made a note in my journal about what he said.

July 30, 2001—Journal entry

I read an interesting article in the Gleaner dated July 27, 2001 and I just had to write this down.
"For the 25-five years old Simpson, it all started eight years ago when he was a member of the Manning Cup team of a prominent high school in Kingston. He

met a man, a strong supporter of the team, he said, and who would later have a profound impact on his life.

According to Simpson, they both took an instant liking to each other and before long the man started to shower him with gifts. "I was a star player on the team and he treated me like one," Explained Simpson. "He gave me clothes, money and basically anything he felt I would be in need of. I never thought anything wrong of it because during my tenure as a football player, I had seen enough pampering of star athletes by over zealous supporters."

...When pressured further, Simpson laughingly admitted that "it felt like courtship" and that he felt an instant chemistry with his newfound friend.... Simpson said that he knew since age ten that he was gay and had his first real encounter with a man six years later. "There was no penetration, it was strictly oral sex. It didn't last, though, he wasn't really my type."

I recently researched and found the article; Simpson fell in love with the man and never had consensual sex with him until after age twenty-one. He ended the relationship as he got quite close to the man's family; the article was titled "*I was sleeping with husband and father*". I questioned whether during the actual courtship was it considered to be abuse? I leave you the reader to judge. The part where he had oral sex is sexual abuse. I assume.

Jamaicans are natural athletes and we do well at the sports we perform. During athletic summer training camps, boys are sometimes molested by their coaches and some never seem to want to talk (information given by a young athlete, who reside I the U.S.). They channel the anger they feel from the abuse and put that energy towards the sports and give of their best. The annual Penn Relay, which is held at Philadelphia in the US, is a common ground for gay Jamaicans. Most of these athletes may never admit that they have been sexually molested by their coaches but I must point out that it does happen. Now I am not saying that it happen to every boy but it does happen. These are practices that occur in society more often than we think or even admit to ourselves. I now ask that we think about all that has been said and have open discussions with your kids. Its not easy to ask some questions, but it is important that as parents you tackle the abuse in its early stage, the later you wait the more difficult it will be for your child to heal.

15

Confusion

o o o o o o o o o o o o o o o o o o o o o o o o o o o o o o o

Someone was hurt before you;
Wronged before you;
Hungry before you;
Frightened before you;
Beaten before you;
Humiliated before you;
Raped before you;
Yet, someone survived.

—*Maya Angelou*

Entering the gates of the University of the West Indies, Mona was one of my greatest achievements in my life. I was like a king, I decided then that I was going to make a name, and ensure that by the time I was finished, my name would have been engraved somewhere in the history of the University for making a positive contribution to the institution for which I did. I organized a tourism society on campus and even though it failed in the end, my name was set in the history of the University. I was renowned for my views and I was never scared to say how I felt about issues that I was passionate about. With all, the greatness to come from the University, I had my first nervous breakdown there and I was convinced that I ought to have been admitted to a mental institution.

For both my first and second years I resided one of the University's most prestigious places of residence, and to my surprise, despite the scenery of the property, it brought about pain and undue stress. The hall was located, just minutes away from, August town, the community where I was molested as a child. I had sleepless nights and I tossed and turned in my bed constantly. The drinking became more intense and I saw failure for the first time. I strongly believe that everything that happen in life happens for a reason and God sent me to this place, to deal with my past. Age is just a number. I looked mature, I was at the age where I should be able to express myself, but what I had deep within me for years could not come out that easy. There are many times I have said to myself, if only I knew, I could have gotten help, and may be, who knows life could have been much easer. By the end of my second semester I had failed four of my five courses and that was it for me. I cried endlessly and no one could calm me down, I begged for my mother but when she decided to come for me I told her not to. But if only she had been a mother and come despite me saying no, maybe things would have turned out much better for me.

I made a meaningful effort to forget all that was going on in my life. Campus was diverse and to my surprise, the gay guys on campus were not few but many and the more obvious and outspoken ones were from the other Caribbean islands. I despised them to the bone. At that time in my life I hated the fact that two men could find pleasure with each other. The truth was to unfold it self to me when I spoke to this guy who had eyes on me. I must say, campus drink up was more than just a drink up; it was a safe haven for gay men who preyed on straight men. I frequented most, if not all campus drink ups, everywhere the drum beat, I had to be there, even if it meant that I had to go by myself. One late night after a drink up was close to ending; I met this guy whom I felt was a bit too friendly with me. He was from Barbados and it was my opinion that Barbados was the gay capital of the British West Indies. He was drunk and he told me in no uncertain terms that he wanted to have sex with me. I was petrified at that time about what he suggested and dismissed him at once. Two days later I saw him, and walked away from him, but he came towards me nonetheless and said that he wanted to apologize for what he did the other night. I must note being drunk is no excuse for committing any sexual act or doing wrong. It is my belief that what a man does in his drunken state it was deep in his subconscious mind and he uses drunkenness as an excuse to do it. He informed me that the night he saw me he got raped, he found himself the next morning in a strange bed with a man next to him. I immediately felt that he was lying as how can a grown man get raped, hell no that could not be possible. It took the hard way for me to find out that truth myself.

He later informed me that while the crimes were never reported, it was a common scene on campus, many nights men would find themselves in strange beds, even their own at times, with men next to them or find themselves in pools of blood. The mere thought of reporting it, will take away their manhood so they keep quiet. With all this rage and anger and them questioning themselves if they are gay because the act has been committed, they try to have sex with as many girls as possible to prove that they are still men. It is my opinion that there is a direct correlation to the raping of women, the physical abuse that women faced on campus and the actual fact that men are being raped and they are venting their anger on these innocent women. Is it rape because a man is over twenty-one and he had a curious mind? Is it rape if he was drunk and was not fully conscious? Is it rape if in his drunken state he never said no? The definition of a sexual act, means that, who ever is engaging in the sexual act must first consent and if the person is drunk, they are not in a frame of mind to consent and if someone says no, no means no. Oddly enough these men would never come forward and talk about these crimes, and even if they did, the laws of my country does not protect them, as nowhere in the laws does it refers to men being raped.

Homosexuality in Jamaica is deemed illegal and punishable with imprisonment with hard labor for up to ten years. There is an irony within all this. It is the intellectual within the country who upholds this law as they are the ones in Government, they were mostly educated at the University of the West Indies, yet it is commonly alleged that so many of our politicians and intellectuals are homosexuals. A distinguished professor from the University once said that "homosexuality is an intellectual disease and most who walk within the gates of the University may never catch it." It was no open secret that quite a few lecturers were gay, but within the Jamaican social context, if you're gay and educated, we need you so its OK, if you're wealthy and gay, its OK as we need your money. If you are a poor man who has not much to offer to society you should not be gay, you must be condemned. Its called double standards and it plays itself out in how our laws are written and how we treat men and women unequally.

After this new knowledge was given to me, I set out on a mission, I wanted to know if there was a direct correlation between getting raped and becoming a homosexual. I had nowhere to start, who I should turn to, without a question mark being placed on my sexuality. I have always been tagged as a homosexual as I never supported the bashing of gay men and I was more open and liberal with my thoughts. Let me stop for a bit, as that statement is a blatant lie, I used to bash those boys who acted feminine and those who I felt were gay, not knowing, that I was merely seeing a reflection of me in them. To this day I have tried to apologize to those guys for whom I have caused so much hurt and pain, but I was young and I never understood what they were going through. I had made several attempts to visit the campus health center to seek help, well personal help, as I needed to talk to someone but I was always scared.

I constantly questioned my sexuality and while I never openly condemned those who I knew were gay, I avoided being in their space, I knew for a fact that I was not prepared for the answer. I had something more important to accomplish and that was getting a degree. In my second year after visiting the rest of the Caribbean islands without stepping foot on them (having sex with women from different islands), I fell in love. It was a match made in heaven and I felt that she was the one. With all the confusion going on in my mind, I needed security and I felt that I could find it only in a woman. I wanted to forget the rape; the possible thought of being gay out of my mind and being with a woman was the only solution to solve the problem. I must say, it is not the way to go, as deep down we still need answers and its not fair to these women. Yes we love them, but we can't fully love them, as there is a part of that is not ready to open up and tell them about the true us, out of fear of rejection. Sure most times we want to, but rejection is not easy, the thought of a woman calling man a homosexual is harder than if a man told him that he is. I had a constant battle with loving this woman and finding a way to deal with the questions I needed answers for. These are my personal thoughts about her and how I battled with depression without her even knowing, which is common in most men who have been raped who disguise their anger by being with a woman.

26.04.2000

I spoke to Natasha yesterday. I am convinced that I need her. I don't think that I am in love but my feelings for her is very deep, I must say. I wanted her badly last night so much. I should not have even seen her as it is a huge distraction, but to hell with it. I am not looking for anything-short term. What is her position, how does she feel about me? Right now I hope she was here, to comfort me. She is all that I need now.

27.04.2000

I finally got the truth; Natasha is playing no game and most of all she was upset about the email I had sent her telling her good bye. She is confused as myself. As the days go by I want her more.
He called tonight, playing games as usual, and asking a lot of mother fucking questions about you know what. I have another kill in mind but I don't know if I should go ahead with the plan.

30.04.2000

My life is getting more and more complicated as the days go by. I did something I promise myself never to do and that was to get myself too involved with Natasha other from what happen the other night, we started making love to each other. Her lips were moist as our lips came together. I enjoy having her tongue in my mouth as if she was trying to take away my soul. Her inner lips were wet with her love juice. I allowed only my index finger to work my way around her clit and move inside of her warm and filled with more love juice. I gently took off her undergarment and gently massage my tongue around her clit, but her pubic hair was too much. Nevertheless, I tasted her love juice; even after she left I could still taste her on my lips. She left me a note a days later saying:

31.04.2000 2:53am

> "Kissing you was like
> Entering a Hershey's warehouse
> And leaving with a single kiss
> Leaving all the other goodies behind
>
> I like your technique
> It has the signals of
> A good lover
>
> Yet I stand
> Then turn my back
> Away from this horizon"

I did something that I should never have done and that was to giver Natasha a copy of *Just as I am* by E. Lynn Harris to read. She was more open to its context as in her country the attitude towards homosexuality were not as severe as Jamaica and that gave me a sense of comfort. My life became more complicated as the unthinkable happened early one morning. It was this guy who I felt was gay in my first year and eventually we developed a mutual friendship. We never spoke about sexuality it was always about school. One night he came to my room and borrowed my VCR and I loan it to him. A few days after I got this tape for a book I was reading for history class and I decided to ask him if I could watch the tape in his room and he said yes. He left me there that night and seeing that the movie was long and I was making notes, I had stopped the tape on several occasions. He came back early the morning and saw me in his bed still, he wanted to sleep and I told him to just lay in the bed, which he did face turn away from me. Something strange happen to me, I moved my leg and I felt a bulge and out of curiosity I moved my leg again to ensure that it was not his penis and sure it was. The third time I moved it I felt a hard penis, which made me know that he was not sleeping, so I asked him what was that I was feeling and said he "what do you think". I moved my leg again, he took it out and within seconds I had this huge ten inch penis in my hand and eventually we were in the 69 position have oral sex and though it was scary, I enjoyed every moment of it. I was twenty years old and this was my first consensual sexual act with a man. After we ejaculated I left feeling embarrassed about what I did. The next day I could not look at him.

06.05.2000

I now hated what happen, it should never have. Why must I intend to fuck around peoples head and leave them all by themselves, out in the dark and cold, having no idea what to do or where or who to turn to. Questions are everywhere, but who is there to answer them. Am I becoming one of them? I should think not, I now hate myself for pushing what happen. I will be leaving in a couple of days and hope that I will not be forced into another position such as the one I was in a couple of minutes ago. 4:56am.

The following night we saw each other and he said that he was ashamed and it was the first time he was doing anything like that. He said he could not explain why he did it and oddly enough he wants to experience it again. He was able to express himself on paper, I allowed him to write in my journal.

07.05.2000

Confusion

How do we find out about ourselves? Who are we? What are we sent here to do? Questions if we knew the answers, we would all be perfect. However this is life, not a dream. Our lives here on earth revolves around what we do. And what we do depends on who we are, and what we try. Sushi doesn't taste good until you find the fish you like. But you keep trying till you do. Puzzles of the mind. What bogs down our natural instincts and reaction to things life surprises us with. We display submissiveness, interests are fulfilled, we in our human nature are confused. Confusion without solution is the greatest problem. However, having fulfilled interest now inspires experimentation.
—Gary Hugh

He was not the only one confused, I enjoyed what happen, but out of innocence it felt much better with Natasha than when I did it with Gary. Nothing much came out of it as I had a girl I was overly in love with and he too was involved. Then we felt that even if the desire to pursue it was strong we would fight them, but not for long. My woman left for the summer and I pleased my curious mind one last time before I journey to New York for the summer. I felt an empty void inside of me and oddly enough I yearned for Gary much more than how I yearned for my girl and then I knew I had to find answers to my questions. My final year brought me more than answers, it changed my life.

After that first sexual encounter on campus I was petrified and I was more confused than ever about my sexual orientation. I could not even otter the word gay from my mouth as nothing in the world could convince me that I was gay. At one point I felt as though I was loosing my sanity and sometimes for days I would shut myself up in my room and refuse to see the outside world. I would drink and even vomit on myself and live in the mess. I was searching for answers, answers to questions that I wasn't too sure I needed to hear the answers to. Drinking was all I could do; it eased the pain, it numb my soul and it created my own elusion of what I thought life ought to be. In my mind I was a heterosexual male but deep within my soul I could not accept that fallacy. I was gay and I had to come to terms with that reality. To this day I have no clue what a gay man ought to be like as I still enjoy the company of women and I do dream about children. Most of all I am not with either sexes for sex, its more intimate or personal than those on the outside would believe.

The journal entries below reflect my frame of mind and how confused I was at age twenty. Here I give you the reader the opportunity to feed into my mind and see the person I was then and how much I battled with dealing with my true identity.

June 29, 2000

I believe that I am gay, not fully but somewhere there. I don't have a lover, thank God for that and my ass is still tight. But somewhere there, I honestly think that I am, I just think about the wrong mother f____king things at the wrong time. I could not stand the pain of anyone f____king my ass, I must say. But the idea of two men eloping brings…let me not say, nonetheless f____k that.

July 21, 2000

Guess what? I did something that I have always wanted to do and I finally got the courage to do it, f____k all those who don't like it. Wait!! I haven't said what it is yet, o yes I pears my ears, yes both of them and it look darn good. My mother will go mad when she sees them. Now can you believe what just happen, daddy, then in my life, the f____king father who was lost all these years, the authoritarian, blasted me for doing it. I know he does not like it but who the hell cares.

August 20, 2000

I am finally on my way home to Jamaica, the week in New York was wonderful, I didn't even want to go home. The last weekend with my brother wasn't bad, the club could have been better but I enjoyed myself. I am going to miss my brother and two sisters, it was my first time seeing them and I don't know if I will ever seem them again.

August 23, 2000

I am home, horny like f____k, but what can I do, nothing. I am glad that I am home but to an extent I wish that I could have stayed. My last week in New York I jump the turnstile and had to pay a fine of $60.00 and I had to buy a one-way ticket home.

I enjoy being online using AOL. I met so many people, in particular two gay teenagers, 16 and 18 who wanted to f___k this tight ass so badly, do you believe them? They mad. The younger one was so hot, one night when I spoke to him, he wanted us to have phone sex, couldn't do that, not me.

I am depraved sexually and there is nothing that I can do about it. I still masturbate as mush as I use to, but I am a grown man and I need to find myself some fine pussy that I can really call my own.

September 06, 2000

I am on the verge of leaving the University. I am so fed up and upset with life itself. I am in the mood for trouble. I am more confused. I live nowhere and I need a room. I am so sorry that I came back home. My mind is ever where lost in the open sand, with no one to turn to. I need some peace of mind, my head pains, my foot hurts what else can I do?

September 21, 2000

I am 20 years old, I sometimes forget my age, but I am young. Tonight I went to bed without any food at all. I have in a very long time felt some hunger that I have not felt in a very long while. I am broke with no money and nothing to do with myself. I am lost. I am in my room most of the times; lock up, with nothing to do. I am overly confused, what the f___k am I going to do with myself. I am hardly going to classes and I am constantly depressed, it is as if I am lacking something, not pussy, could get that if I wanted, not love, I don't even know what I want.

September 30, 2000

The days are going quickly—I will be out of this mother f__king place sooner than I had thought, thank God. I need some form of shelter, someone or something to cover me. I have sinned against God and come short of his glory—I fuck, let me not even explain, I regretted doing it, fuck this is not the life I wanted, it isn't a matter of want or need. I have no mother fucking idea of what is going on, in my life. I now hate going down that mother f__king place. That is over, but I am thinking too much about it and that is my problem. Others are even fucking around me, this is one circle I which not to be apart of. Fuck!! I am on Taylor Hall and if this gets out I would have to kill my fucking self. I hope I won't have to go there.

October 04, 2000

Hunger has now become a concept to me. It is fucking hard, but this is the harsh reality of my life. My sister spoke to me yesterday, we got upset with each other because she wanted me to do the impossible, which was to distress myself, I can't.

Let me change the subject there is this young man I went to school with. I know that he is gay. I have avoided him deliberately. Well he has for a couple of weeks been trying o make what I <u>think</u> is a pass at me. He was brave enough a couple of nights ago to ask me why I was avoiding him or was it that I was just unfriendly to him. You should know me I was fucking upset. I told him that it was me; I was an introvert most of the times.

The reality of the situation is that each time I look at this Youngman there is a question mark. I know myself I am overly curious, and it is this curiosity that may lead me to want to know what that huge question mark means. He knows something about me and I need to find out what it is. The reality is that I want him more than ever. It may happen if I play my cards right, for which I intend to do. Anything I want I must fucking get. I am overly confused; I don't know what I want. He (the guy who rape me at 14) have been calling me quite often, that mo fucka is looking something believe it or not.

January 1, 2001

I am lost in the world filled with hate and lies. My life is filled with shit, things I am hiding from, things that are so fucking hard to talk about. I have been through so much pain, lost and hurt. I am filled with anger. I need to be loved, to be cared for someone who will hold me in their arms and let me let go of some of these shit that is killing me so deep inside.

February 09, 2001

Believe me life can be f..ked up at times and in most instances we are the ones responsible for fucking ourselves. A couple days ago, I thought that I was going mad, when _____ called to tell me that she was infected and that she has an STS and I need to go get tested. I will hear what my life has to offer me on Tuesday of this week. So far life is good and I am physically in good health. The bitch lied, it wasn't me, and she was fucking with another man.

February 14, 2001

The older I get the more and more life gets complicated. Everyday we learn more and more about others and ourselves around us. I just found out that a friend of mine is gay. I can't believe that she could be gay, hell no. I saw Darnel today. I wonder if we could meet up at some other point in life not as lover but as friends and express our deep feels without getting involved sexually. If I were gay I would want him all for myself, to be all mines. When will someone try to understand these people and realize that they are people like any one else. Heterosexual don't even understand that they are the ones who force them to be who they are. They are so many reasons why someone would want to become gay. Failed relationships, forced into sex at an early age

March 1, 2001

Today is my day, it actually comes only once per year. I am finally 21yrs old and I have so much to be thankful and grateful for. I have been blessed over a thousand times and I must say thanks to my creator. I need to let go of so much things and start all over. In a couple of weeks I will complete my first degree and hopefully start my life on a new leaf.

March 7, 2001

Lost is not the word to describe how I feel. I feel light headed as if I am loosing something. It is as if I am here only to pass time. My legs are constantly week, my brain seem exhausted and can no longer retain any fucking thing. I feel as if I am in a world all by myself. My social skills are now lacking, I need some pussy that is what I fucking need.

I think to some extent that I am scared of being me, scared of living and gaining the independence that I truly need. I am not and will never be accepted by those around me. I am constantly be ridiculed for being who I am.

I want to cry so fucking much and I don't want to do it alone. I need to let it all out. I can feel the tears wanting to come out but it's a man thing. I don't feel man enough to cry and get close to my feelings. Who can I trust? That is so fucking hard to do these last days. At times I feel used, abused and hurt by those I value the most around me. The things that I do are not because I want to do them, but it puts me I a different world, that I can't control. Now I understand why people drink.

March 23, 2001

I am finally getting professional help for my emotional problems. At least I know that one person cares. I met a young batty boy today him cute but too real for me to deal with. Rudjam.com a Jamaican sex site has a lot to offer. I have decided to join the team and if things work out I will be getting some pussy.

16

Fire pan Rome

♦

The Christian Religion and Denomination

○ ○

Religion is the opium of the people

—Kharl Marx

For as long as I can remember Spiderman and Batman as a child there has always been a debate about sexuality and the role of the church. In order to get an in-depth understanding of the role of the church in regards to sexuality and the rape and abuse of boys, it is important to go back into history. I refer to Christian history and slavery, the importation of Christianity and the forced imposition of Christian values on slaves. The British being the Christians they were, they were appalled when they encountered blacks in Africa, who were naked, had a different religion practice and culture beliefs. Based on studies conducted over the years, many African cultures have an explanation and a place for dominant women and even effeminate men. Nudity was common and Africans were comfortable with their sexuality. The ancestors of slaves were not barbarians as Europeans called them and yes they did have a culture, which was more sophisticated and developed than their enslavers.

It is sad that the history of Africa was never taught to blacks in Africa from African perspective and to those of the African Diaspora. Even though slavery in British colonies ended over 250 years ago; blacks of the Diaspora are still traumatized by the aftermath of slavery. As a people we have been hurt, not only by the obvious physical assaults our ancestors had to endure but psychologically as well. One of the legacies of slavery is the damage to the sexuality of those formerly enslaved.

The sad thing is that we tend to talk only about it's effects on women and neglect to examine how it has destroyed black men except when these black men are used as sex objects, for centuries and in doing so the social fabric of the black families. Blacks were never taught their history. This was a history that was diluted and reduced to lies. Those of us—descendants of slavery were all told lies. It is also sad that few of our intellectuals who do know our history still refuse to teach us our history. But, education is power and in the age of capitalism and globalization, who would want a social revolution as Marx's prophesied?

We may never have a revolution nor can we undo what has been done to us as a people. The solution however to all this madness comes only when we are willing to have discussion, open dialog and educate the uneducated. What we are facing today is post-traumatic slavery syndrome and there is no time but the present to start the talking. Let us fool ourselves no more, sexual abuse of black men is real and we are dealing with the repercussions of not dealing with it now with the increase of HIV and AIDS among black men and the spread of these diseases to our black women.

The Church is one group that has mis-educated blacks about African culture. Christianity is nothing but a false imprint on the minds of people, which serves its own immoral values of hatred. The Church claims that it preaches about love and forgiveness yet it's the first to judge and condemn. Christianity over the years has played a fundamental role through its colonial influence to suppress traditional African cultural values and dehumanize the African sexuality. Africans are highly sexual and spiritual people. The gods of Africa were denounced by European colonizers, as were the African sexuality and its appreciation of nudity. It wasn't until Christianity had infiltrated African societies that Africans began to cover them selves. Remember, it was the Christian church who called Africans savages and used the bible as a means to justify slavery.

One cannot talk about spirituality in African traditional societies and not discuss its sexuality, as both come hand in hand. The beating of the drums put anyone of black descendants into a dancing mood. Within the dance moves are evidences of our sexuality.

It wasn't' until the bible was introduced by the colonizers to the Africans that we learned to hate homosexuality. One writer pointed out that, it was the Bible with which the colonizers instilled a deep fear in blacks and used this to justify their hatred of blacks and homosexuality alike.

I grew up condemning homosexuality believing that it was a white man disease. The justification for my dislike was based on my religious belief. I was unable then to quote the verse from the bible that openly condemned homosexual acts. It is not surprising that almost all Jamaicans and blacks across the Diaspora have become confused with the notion that homosexuality was introduced to blacks by the colonizers and of the same notion that Africans were totally ignorant of such acts until it was brutally forced on them during slavery. I should point out that it is a fact that homosexuality as an act was forced on many slaves, to keep them in submission and by this practice was passed from generation to generation through the ages. The sad thing is that slavery has ended and our own men are still raping our boys. The notion that Africans were totally ignorant of homosexuality within their culture before slavery was introduced is far from the truth. In fact it was the other way around, blacks were more sexually open and the British were the "tight assed moralist".

While searching the Internet for information regarding homosexuality in Africa, I found Erilou statement on a Nigerian news website. According to the president of Alliance Rights Nigeria, a gay organization, homosexuality has always existed in Africa. Erilou says that "In some cultures in the northern parts of Nigeria, there are people called *dan doudy* which is a typical *Housa pseudonym*—It means men who are wives of men. In the old days, to show your immense wealth it was easy to have a haven of wives. But to show that you were truly rich, you had to keep a stable man. You had to take care of your *dan doudu* and their family". He further states that these wealthy men would have sexual relationships with the *don doudu*. "What else is homosexuality"?

In contemporary and African history, little or no time is allocated to the discussion of sexuality in Africa. Eugene J. Patron, *Heart of Lavender: In Search of Gay Africa* Harvard Gay and Lesbian Review, Fall 1995, gives compelling information based on research on the prevalence of homosexuality in Africa. As with most societies, which had to face the imprint of colonialism on its societies, Africans too claimed that homosexuality was attributed to the legacy of European and Arab colonialist. Patron supported his claims by making reference to the 1991 trial of Winnie Mandela who was convicted of kidnapping and murdering a 14-year-old boy. Mandela defended herself both in court and in the press by arguing that she was merely trying to protect a number of local youths from "the homosexual overtures of white priest." Sure, Mrs. Mandela has a valid point but such a point can only hold grounds, if presented within the context that homosexuality was not a direct imprint of European colonization. Patron continues in his article that there is a growing body of evidence to support a biological root to homosexual behavior. There, he claims is substantial evidence to argue that homosexuality is innate in all race and cultures. The article further notes that while homosexual desire may be innate to only a percentage of a population the opportunities to express such desires are clearly regulated by cultural boundaries. Patron gave two samples of his studies in the article. He spoke of Azande-which is present day Zaire.

Most traditional African cultures are based upon extended family structures and are evident throughout Jamaican societies. Patron points out that anthropologist place homosexuality in direct opposition to procreation. Homosexualities viewed from a purely economic perspective suggest that a society must determine the choice of an individual not to have children. The economic interdependence of members of an extended family or clan is a deterrent to homosexuality and is seen as an issue relating to behavior and not desire. The article states that, there is anthropological evidence showing that a number of African cultures possess a degree of accommodation towards homosexuality. Evans-Pritchard is noted in the article for his study on the exploration of homosexuality in Africa beginning in the 1920s. Based on Patron article, Evans-Pritchard found repeated examples of adolescents prior to the age of 17-18 serving as "boy wives" to older men. They were expected to help their "fathers-in-law" and "mothers-in-law" to cultivate the fields, build huts and would often sleep with their fathers-in-law. According to the evidence presented by Evans-Pritchard "if a Azande man has sexual relations with a boy he is not unclean. The Azande says. 'A boy does not pollute the oracle.' " "Moreover the boy wife and his father-in-law would often refer to each other "my love" and "my lover". Further readings of boy wives in Africa can be found in *Boy-Wives and Female-Husbands: Studies of African Homosexuality* by Stephen O' Murray.

Patron argues that one of the best-documented cases of homosexuality in African is found among the mineworkers of South Africa. The workers were living in male compounds and separated from their wives and girlfriends for months, the article states that it was very common for adolescent boys to visit these compounds and provide sexual services to these men. Such acts of homosexuality can be considered as situational homosexuality, based upon the extenuating circumstances of an all male setting. It was pointed out in the study that consideration must be given to those miners and their partners who admit to enjoying sexual contacts with other men beyond obtaining sexual release in the absence of their women.

What I found more interesting of the cases in the cases presented in Patron's article was of the study conducted by Linda Ngcobo and Hugh McLean in *Defiant Desires* who interviewed twenty African men, who have had sex with other men, about gay sexuality in the township of Johannesburg. Ngcobo explained some terms "A *skesana* is a boy who likes to get fucked." "An *injonga.*" is the one who makes the proposal and does the fucking" The article continues to note that anal sex is far from unknown, and that the definition of sex between men is only when there is anal penetration.

Yes, it is a fact that European men did sexually abused men within their colonies and it is also a given fact that homosexuality existed among the colonizers themselves as pointed out in *Colonialism and Homosexuality* by Robert Aldrich.

A rather interesting article in *New Africa*, February, 2004. No. 426 written by Stella Orakwue on History's' Most Sordid Cover-up, she argues, the mass rape of black women by white men during the colonial period is history's greatest shame. It is sad that when talking about sexual abuse and slavery we still refuse to talk about how white men use to R.A.P.E black men to keep them submissive. Stella further argued that men could not protect these women; she even questioned, "What is a man who cannot protect his woman and children from attack from other men?" My question to her is what is a man who cannot even protect himself from another man, what does his woman think of him when his manhood is ripped away from him? It wasn't easy for black men during slavery, I strongly believed that they wanted to protect they families but it was even more difficult to protect themselves from a system of oppression. We need to be more balanced in our discussion of the implication of slavery with regards to sexual abuse as it affected both men and women.

While homosexuality can be discussed from a pure biological perspective, the cultural aspect of sexuality should not be ignored. The editor The *Many Faces of Homosexuality*, Anthropologist Evelyn Blackwood, quoting from her peers Rapp and Ross, said that "sex feels individual, or at least private, but those feelings always incorporate the roles, definition, symbols and meanings of the worlds in which they are constructed".

Religion has had a profound effect on most traditional African societies and it has become transformed throughout most of the African Diaspora. *Voodoo* as a religion also has its origins deep within traditional African societies and while voodoo is not prevalent within Jamaican societies something similar exist called *Obeah*. Obeah, practiced in Jamaica and many of the English speaking Caribbean communities, takes the form of knowledge of ancient nature worship originally handed down over the centuries by oral tradition from the remnants of a once powerful and celebrated religious order, which is now lost in time. It was practiced mainly by the tribal people who spoke Ashanti from West Africa—Sorcery (Voodoo) and witchcraft. The practice of obeah is conducted by an *Obeah-Man* or a *Obi-Man*. Zola Hurston gives a compelling account of obeah in her novel *Tell my Horse: Voodoo and life in Haiti & Jamaica* 1938. Hurston gives a compelling account of a nine-night ceremony and how a dead man spirit transformed a man into a zombie.

To understand the symbolism in the spirit world within the African culture I will attempt to explore Patron discussion of traditional Zulu culture were women were spirit diviners. Due to the fact that females are able to give birth, it is through their bodies that spirit may cross from one world to another. Within the Zulu culture men who display female gender characteristics were allowed to be spirit diviners. When a spirit possesses a person, no matter what the gender identity, the spirit is considered to be a woman. From what I have known and heard while growing up in Jamaica, most if not all obeah men are homosexuals. A friend once told me about an incident with an obeah man when he was about thirteen years old and he was given a bath by the obeah man. When the man was using his oils to anoint him, and washing his body he manually masturbated my friend. I have heard similar stories of spiritual dances and men dancing together with erect penises. I am not claiming that homosexuality is a part of the spiritual practice of obeah ritual, what I am saying is that it is incidental to the practice.

Slavery is over and done with, yet blacks are still in a state of mental enslavement. We use the bible, the book of life, which was the tool used to claim that slavery was justifiable in the eyes of God and now claimed that homosexuality is wrong. Church members can be considered a bunch of hypocrites because one of the best hiding ground for homosexuals is in the church. The virulent condemnation of homosexuality has forced many homosexuals within the church to prey on young boys, since they are unable to make their advances on adult men. Most boys that I have interviewed for this book were either molested or raped by a pastor or some male from within the church. While these young boys are forced into engaging in sexual acts, each week during the sermon, the pastor would talk openly and candidly about God's will and his condemnation of the homosexual act. As a child I looked up to my pastor and believed every word he said, since I also believed that he was a man of God. I know how these young boys felt, being forced to have sex with these men, after church or during weekly church meetings.

The church has had profound influence on the cultural beliefs of Jamaicans, which in turn has influenced their thought processes. Like most black communities, absentee fathers plague the Jamaican society, and single mothers find it very difficult to raise young boys by themselves. The church becomes a refuge for these mothers and most times these boys are left in the hands of the males within the church. These males are given the responsibility to protect, guide and teach these young boys how to be men. Rather than give these young boys the love and affection that they yearn so much, they are brainwashed, coerced. The supposedly upstanding men seduce these boys into engaging in sex with them. Out of fear, of being condemned and being accused of lying, these boys are forced to keep silent and hide themselves even further in the church. They live with the pain and guilt of wanting to speak up but feel trapped because of the laws of God. One young man explained to me that when he was a choirboy the head deacon who was in charge of the youth choir use to have sex with him. Each Thursday he was asked to come in earlier for service. The reader is encouraged to use your imagination and think about what supposedly Godly service this "man of God" could be doing to this young boy.

I do believe that the role of the church is still to provide love, comfort and solace for those in need. The church is not a place were poor people go to put down their burden, it is a place where grown men who are scared of accepting who they are prey on young boys. Most closeted gay men have some important standing in church. The abuse continues for years on end, and more and more young boys are drawn into the arms of these men. Many of those boys who were molested sometimes grow up to be molesters themselves. For some it has become a part of their mental buildup.

It is painful to listen to a pastor who openly condemns homosexuality yet after church he has sex with selected boys of the Church in the name of God. Jamaican churches are filled with hypocrites. Those who have no clue about the interpretation of the bible, yet in the church they talks of love and yet, they are the first to cast out a brother if he is found out to be a homosexual. As an example, the church also preaches about forgiveness, yet the pastors and the older folks are the first to judge and cast stone. I have read the bible and the New Testament states that, any man who is without sin should cast the first stone if he feels he is sinless and because we have all come into the world as sinners, we don't have the right to cast any stones. Some Christians even allude that God was responsible for writing the laws in the bible that states that homosexuality is wrong. Honestly, I don't believe that the practice of raping boys within black churches will end until as a people blacks begin to accept and come to terms with the fact that it does happen, and if we continue to hide from the truth there will be detrimental consequences later in life for many of the abused boys.

Some consequences thus far have manifested them selves, as the rates of black women with HIV are on the rise. In some cases, men within the church openly sleep with men, become infected with the HIV virus and because HIV and AIDS is considered a homosexual disease not only in Jamaica but the world over, most men never get tested. They themselves don't even consider themselves gay as they have wives and kids. Some of these infected men abuse young boys within the church or community and also infect them with the virus. These young boys even those abused do not relate to the homosexual life style and openly have unprotected sex with women who then become infected.

The church as an institution has failed the ones who they claim to protect. According to the bible, in its first book, the book of Geneses 19; 1-38, it speaks about Sodom and Gomorrah and the eventual destruction of these cities with no clear correlation to homosexuality. Homosexuality is a contemporary term and there is no Hebrew or ancient Greek equivalent. It was a Hungarian writer who coined the word towards the second half of the 19th century. Then, the word did not appear in the English language until the end of the 19th century. Evidence exist that the first use of the term homosexual in an English bible did not come about until 1946, with the publication of the Revised Version of the New Testament. It is a misconception and it is misleading for Christians to suggest that the account of the destruction of Sodom and Gomorrah was because the people of the city were wicked and their wickedness was based on a homosexual orientation. Now for those bigots, who use the Bible as a shield to justify the crucifixion of homosexuals, the word "Sodomite" has no direct correlation to the word "Sodom" or "Sodomy". Although "Sodomite" is written in some English translation of the bible, no Hebrew or Greek word is formed on the name "Sodom" or ever appeared in the biblical manuscripts on which those versions were based. It is argued that the Old Testament attacks male prostitution not because they engage in same sex relation but rather because they served more than one gods, which is a sin based on one of the Ten Commandments—Thou shall have no other gods before me.

It is also necessary to stop using the argument of Adam and Eve. Not all married couple can have children so should they not have sex, since sex for them is exclusively for pleasure?. What about women, who are unable to conceive, should they too not have sex as they are unable to fulfill the Genesis command, "Be fruitful and multiply" or should the church claim that these women have been cursed by God. If the church as it claims speaks the truth about the Bible, these men within the church will stop preying on these young boys. HIV and AIDS may not come directly from the church, but people within our churches do have the virus and help to spread it. As a people we have yet to embrace sexually transmitted disease and as a nation we need to be more aggressive about educating people about HIV and AIDS. May be and I do say may be, if the church was more accepting of the reality, then may be, some men will be more honest to themselves and stop from molesting boys. The Church ought to take responsibility for the actions of its members and it needs to help open up the minds of its members so that they are not lead a stray by the teachings of a church who has incorporated the messages of the Colonial oppressors. Jamaican churchgoers are living in a lie and the deception that the country is homophobic, is all a facade. Should night could turn to day, we would see for ourselves the amount of men who are out preying on young boys or engaging in homosexual acts. The absence of openness has forced our men to abuse young boys, which in turn contributes to the destruction of the future generation of men.

In my eyes, homosexuality is no sin and from my understanding of the Bible gives no condemnation of the sexual act and if so it is not the greatest of all sin. All sin is spelled SIN and Jesus says that the worst sin of all is the unforgivable sin of blasphemy, against the Holy Sprit. So watch out all you Christians, you may have bought a one-way ticket to hell. The apostle Paul included LYING, GLUTLONY, DRUNKNESS, GOSSIPING, FITS OF RANGE and REVELRY among the sins that result in eternal damnation. For those Jamaicans reading, the Catholic Church isn't the only church that molests young boys, it happens in almost every church on that small island we call home. I have often times ask myself why these young boys should have to face their molesters each week, the constant rebuke of the same act they commit each week.

When will it end? Which one of the young men will be brave enough to come out and try to put a stop to all this madness? When will our men stop hiding under the cloak of the church and commit these acts of brutality among our young men? Who will protect them? I leave you the reader to think on what I have said and invite you the reader to take the time to reflect on my words and the role and function of the church in today's society. Our men are hurting and we as a community need to put a stop to it. The church needs to regroup and come clean; I do believe it is still a sacred institution. I leave you the reader with a letter addressed to a pastor from a young boy and the pastors' response and ask you to judge for yourself if more of our boys will continue to be raped and molested within our church and will their cries and pain left ignored.

The Jamaican Star
Teen with homosexual feelings

December 19, 2001

Dear Pastor,
I am a teenager and I am plagued with this problem of homosexuality. I know that homosexual behavior is condemned by the Lord. Some of those who practice it do not condemn it. It is their lifestyle. But I do not want to continue to practice homosexuality. I feel terrible about it.

I am very popular and many girls love me but I do not have a girlfriend. I do not have any feelings at all for women. Many people believe that I have a girlfriend because I am a handsome guy.

Just by looking at the pants front of guys make me feel aroused and I want to have sex with them. I want to stop doing these things.

Sometimes I do crazy things in my bedroom. There are many homosexuals around me. Nobody is helping each other to stop. I want to be a good Christian.

So please help me by giving me the name of a doctor I can talk to. I do not know who to trust. I do not want to condemn. Please pray for me.

Dear…,

I believe that you are genuinely seeking help, but whether so or not, it would do you no good to condemn you. You mentioned the area you are living and that many homosexuals are there. Some of the things you mentioned should not be published and I surely would not want to put any such thoughts in the minds of anyone, especially young men. It seems to me that the area in which you are living can be described as little Sodom and Gomorrah.

Most studies have shown that homosexual behavior is learned. You wish to stop practicing homosexuality. I am sure that most Christians would gladly pray for you. Many people do say that it is not possible for practicing homosexuals to stop. However, from time to time we read the testimonies of many who give glory to God for delivering them from the curse of homosexuality. They claim that they are no longer homosexuals. They say that they have been delivered by the grace of God.

I know of a psychiatrist who is a Christian and he has told me that he has been able to help homosexuals. One such person is now happily married and living a victorious Christian life. I believe therefore, that there is hope for you. I am sure the same psychiatrist would be happy to meet with you.
Pastor

17

Seeking help

o o o o o o o o o o o o o o o o o o o o o o o o o o o o o o o
*"I'd like to be perfect, but instead I
have to settle for being a flawed human
being attempting to learn life's trick lessons".*

—*Halle Berry.*

I strongly believe that the greatest give of all is to give to someone less fortunate than your self. I have never considered myself a victim as such as I was always scared of letting anyone know that I was sexually abused. Separate and apart from forming an organization on campus, I decided to joint a mentoring group who help kids after school with their schoolwork. It was important for me to join, as I wanted to show the true meaning of helping kids without taking advantage of them. I had the privilege of helping two little girls, one 11 years old and the other 12.

I had so much fun with them both and I was always eager to see them. On the few days that I was unable to see them they would get angry with me. On two occasions they even found my dorm to see what was up with me. The young one was quite advance in terms of her academic capabilities and somewhat more of a tomboy as she had more fun time playing games with the boys. The older one changed my life as we had so much in common, no matter what I did to help her, her grades still remained low. There was some gradual improvements but I knew that there was something going on and I had all the intentions in the world to figure out what was going on. I decided to get a bit personal, it was hard gaining her trust, but eventually I did.

I encouraged her to write as she had a problem expressing herself so I felt it best that she should write down her thoughts. She was a bit hesitant at first as like myself she had a huge spelling problem. I told her that a bat could spell better that me and I would ignore her grammar, all she needed to do was write and I would help her correct the spelling. I found out that she was finding it difficult to deal with the death of her grandmother. At that time I was still coping with the death of my grandmother from 1997and was unable to offer much comfort. The saddest part of her story was that she was been sexually abused my her uncle at home, but never knew how to walk away from it and she had nowhere else to go. She pleaded to me to not say anything to anyone and out of trust I kept my promise. Was my actions right or wrong? Not sure only God can judge that. I do however feel that I should have got some help for her.

It was this little girl who gave me the idea to want to form a non-profit organization to help kids who were sexually abused. I am more interested in the educational aspect of it as most times children who are sexually abused are so consumed with the abuse, they lose focus from school and in the end fail. It is my dream to give them some form of help and give them a bit of push. I do hope that by the time the book is published I should be well on the way to form such an organization. This book goes far beyond my story of being sexually abuse; it's an effort to start meaningful conversation on the subject matter and to try save a life.

The first steps in seeking help and heal from childhood sexual abuse, you must believe that you were a victim it is hard to do, but you can do it. When children get abused it becomes dangerous for them to trust their own discernment. It is hard to admit that the same neighbor who helped you with work after school, the neighbor you trusted could force himself on you. It was horrible for me to bear. I pretended for years that it never happened and that it was not abuse, it was love. Many a times we don't think or realize that we have being abused and that is a difficult question to answer. I take a few notes from Ellen Bass and Laura Davis ("Beginning to Heal: A First Book for Survival of Child Sexual Abuse"). As victims, sometimes we are not sure if what we experience is actual abuse and fits the definition of abuse and that is why sometimes we never speak up.

If anyone of these ever happened to you, yes you were sexually abuse.

- Were you ever touched unnecessarily in your private parts?

- Were you forced to touch someone else's private parts?
- Were you made to pose for sexual pictures?
- Were you forced to have oral sex?
- Were you raped or did you have things forced inside your anus?
- Were you fondled or kissed in a way that felt bad to you?
- Were you forced to watch people have sex?
- Were you shown sexual movies?
- Were you told you were only good for sex?
- Were you ridiculed about your body or your sexuality?
- Were you pressured into having sex you didn't really want?
- Were you forced to abuse or hurt someone else?
- Were you forced to take part in rituals that involved violence, sex or torture?

I had always suspected that I was sexually abused when he told me that it was over and that it was just sex and he had a commitment to make to his girlfriend. I never decided to get professional help until it was alleged that I had given the woman I was so much in love with a STD. I got tested twice and still there was no sign of Chlamydia in my system. I was furious with her, as I knew I was faithful to her. When I got tested the second time I was beyond nervous and I shut myself off from the world for the two weeks before I got the result. I was convinced at one point that I had contracted the AIDS virus based on my unprotected sexual activities with my lover when I was fourteen years old. For nine days of the fourteen days I lock myself in my room. I turned off my cell phone, put the T.V on mute and I never answered a knock on my door. I never went to the bathroom until late light, it was an open shower some what and I hated the idea of taking a shower with other men around me. I was in deep depression. I remember wanting to leave the room and I urinated in Pepsi bottles and for days on ends I refused to take a shower, I finally took one on the day I went for the result at the campus health center.

I arrived at the health center early and waited in the waiting room patiently and nervously until my name was called. When my name was finally called, I could hardly walk to get to the doctors office. She saw my anxiety and she quickly told me not to worry, we spoke about STD and how it was impacting campus and to my surprise it was somewhat high, for a population of 70% women. I felt at that point that it was the right moment to seek help. It was a bold step and I took a chance and told the doctor my story and she recommended a psychiatrist I could talk to. She worked for the University and she being on campus would have made traveling much easier for me. Two weeks after the recommendation I got an appointment to see the doctor, I never wanted to go at first as I felt as if I was sick and I needed help. Deep down inside of me I wanted to talk to some one but I had yet to develop the courage or the strength to relive my past.

For the first two visits I never said much, but she recommended that if I were unable to speak, it would be best if I write my thoughts down and it was a lovely suggestion. The pen and paper gave me my own unique voice and until that day I have a journal where I record my worst and fondest moments in my life. After a while I was able to be more open and candid about my experience and the anger I had inside of me. I spoke to her many a time with tears in my eyes, as it was hard to even admit that these things did happen to me. I told her about how I had gotten hooked to the Internet and I was chatting with a lot of young men my age group on campus and around Jamaica who claimed to be gay and I wanted to know if they were rape or molested like myself. I was my own self-research and I needed answers to questions I could never answer and I wanted to know if I was all alone. I was elated when I found these other guys, that was 2000 and I still keep in touch with a few of these men who are gay and living a double life in Jamaica. I told her that a few of the young men were confused and that they were either molested or rape but they all had one thing in common, they refused to go to the police as they fear the embarrassment it would bring about to their families. Now that is some bullshit but it still does occur. I told her about the guy I was developing feelings for but was scared to engage in sex or anything physical with him. She strongly suggested that based on the levels of anger I had within, and my confused state of mind, it was already affecting my grades and I should take a leaf of absence. I could not; I refused to let my troubles break me. Even though I never got an honors degree, I am proud of myself, for fighting a battle that I should never have fought alone.

I fancy going to sit and talk with her every Thursday, I felt a sense of worth each week. She encouraged me to write some more, use the pen as a tool to let my anger out. She reassured me that I was not gay and that what happened to me between my ex lover was wrong; it was a case of abuse. She made it quite clear that a sexual act does not make one gay. Our sessions never lasted long as she had to go on vacation and she left me in the hands of a man. I tried speaking with him, but I never trusted him so I decided not to go back.

My then best friend at the time Morris was curious about where I was going each day and was eager to know. I told him where I was going but I never told him the reasons why I was seeing her. He felt that being my best friend, I should have felt more comfortable talking to him than her as I knew him longer and he would understand. It's the sincerity of him why we were friends for so long. He knew me that well; he knew when I was in pain and when I needed someone to talk to. I trusted this young man with my life. I eventually decided to sit him down one morning and tell him the story from beginning to end with tears in my eyes. He sat there attentively and listened to each word. He never hugged me and he showed no sign of sympathy but yet I knew he felt my pain and understood what I was going through and why I was silent most of the times. I felt cured, if one could say that and it further convinced me not to go see that man who was left to deal with my case. He encouraged me to fight my homosexual urges and that each time it came to mind, I should sit and talk to him. He was all I had as a friend and to an extent he was all I got. With all this information, he later betrayed my trust, turned his back and now we are no longer friends.

Even though I had stop counseling, I still continued to search the Internet looking for more young men like myself. I was not a favorite on campus as they were many who assumed that I was gay but in my mind I wasn't yet actually. They were men who would do everything in their powers just to get in bed with me but I turned them all down. I had developed my own sense of individuality and I was conscious of the way I presented myself. I was looking great then, that summer I had traveled to New York and I work my body out. I had muscles, well toned and a flat chest to die for. My head was now clean shaved and I took great care in how I shaped my beard and mustache. I had taken a risk and pierce my ears and it brought about a greater sex appeal to me. I dressed rather conservative, more imitating European fashion, tight pants, small shirt, a dainty look rather. With my newfound image and confidence, the young gay guys on campus wanted to be with me and they even told lies and made stories about who I had been with. I never cared, as I alone knew the truth and I left them to themselves.

Seeking help in Jamaica about homosexual feelings is rather difficult. One of the major concerns is trust, as we never know who we could trust or even express openly how we felt about our sexuality. I knew how depressed I felt about the way I felt about men and the depression never eased until I had spoken to the doctor. Even though I had ended my sessions with her by choice, she gave me the strength to wanting to get over the depression. I never liked her suggestions but I was determined to get over it. I have lived with depression most of my young and adult life, I have mastered how to hide it and create a facade around others and I have grown to live with it and accept it for what it is, a part of me. I had no clue of what depression meant until I spoke to this woman. Most men who were sexually abuse go through some state of depression even if they admit it or not and they use whatever means possible to ease the pain. My greatest reliever of depression was alcohol and sex. I am happy to say that today I am no longer an alcoholic and I have lessened my sexual encounters.

Most men who are sexually abused never get help and they attempt at living a normal life, with a wife and child. Most young men like my self have refused to seek help and at times this lack of help can destroy marriages and families. We as men can hide our pain and struggles of wanting to get it out of our minds but it is still deep within the surface and needs to be let out. Most men tend to ignore mental pain, some are so sever they won't even take an aspirin for a simple headache. Most men believe in self-medication, which is the worst remedy. The reality of it all is that someday survivors of sexual abuse will have to deal with it and the longer it takes the harder it becomes. The pain does not go away because we simply deny that it exist, in fact it gets worse and in all of that we may even loose ourselves.

I must remind the readers that the book is written within a Jamaican context. Most young men and boys continue to refuse to get help out of shame because of society's refusal to see beyond the sexual act of the abuse. Getting help for these young men has posed a challenge for me and while some may have reported the crimes, what good will that do, as these boys will face more shame and guilt as the police force are not trained to deal with such issues. Sure enough the island is still in denial so it claims that men are sexually abuse but society's actions and attitudes say another.

I may not be the best person to make recommendations for young men who have been sexually abused as I am not a trained professional, but these are just my personal thoughts and suggestions based on my readings. I have somewhat attempted to deal with my past and by writing this book, I have let a huge load off my shoulders and it is a great feeling. It wasn't easy reliving the moments but in the end it was all worth it. Jamaica now faces the problem of many untrained experts who are incapable of dealing with such issues as sexual abuse of men, but we can tackle the issue in a more realistic way. I am not suggesting therapy for everyone, but we can start the journey by first trying to get help, talk to some one who you think you trust and let it all out. You can talk to a trusted friend or a Pastor, a licensed guidance counselor, social worker or a psychologist. I do find talking to strangers rather relieving, well for me talking in general helps, as you are owning up to the realty that the abuse did occur and that is the first step. The second step is to get the notion out of your head that it was your fault or you did something to encourage this to happen to you.

Another great source of getting over the pain of abuse is to find others who have been through similar situations like you. You make not be like me and hunt the Internet in search of abused boys, but over a period of time you may meet up with someone who have been abused and you can share stories with each other it helps, knowing that you are not alone. You can also join a survival group and connect with other survivors. Together as a group, you can learn so much from each other and you may develop skills to help ease the pain. I have tried researching groups in Jamaica that facilitates such a discussion but none exist. Although Jamaica forum for Lesbians, All sexual and Gays (JFLAG) have on several attempts ignored my emails regarding the subject mater, I will recommend that they would be a suited group to deal with such issues.

Urquiza and Crowley (1986), argues that men were more likely to express a desire to hurt others and have a sexual interest in children. This is in correlation to *(Brown & Finkelhor, 1986) Early* and long tern Effects of Child Sexual Abuse: An update. The last finding is very interesting and somewhat controversial, as many men will argue that because of what they had to endure as a child growing up because of sexual abuse, they would wish to molest a child to have them go through what they have been through. Urquiza has been one of very few investigators to ask a sample of victims about their sexual interest in children. The research found that, twenty-five percent of male victims interviewed said that they had some kind of sexual fantasies involving children (vs. 9% of non-victimized men and 3% of the victimized women) and 13% indicated a desire to fondle or engage in sexual activities with a child vs. 6% of non-victimized men. This study strongly supports the hypotheses that male victims may be at higher risk for becoming abusers themselves. While the study may hold some ground, other researchers find the result rather controversial.

Sexual abuse symptoms

In a continuation of David & Finkelhor, 1986 research, the article notes that sexual abuse constitutes a form of posttraumatic stress disorder (PTSD). The report further state that "starting with Gelinas (1983), many articles have appeared making this connection, mostly in anecdotal and clinical ways (Courtors, 1986; Donaldson & Gardner, 1985; Eth & Pynios, 1985; Frederick, 1986; Goodwin, 1985; Lindberg & Distad, 1985) studies suggest that a significant fraction of sexual abuse victims suffer from PTSD—type symptoms (flash-backs, nightmares, numbing of some effects, a sense of estrangement sleep problems) in the immediate aftermath and even longer.

In *No Secrets No Lies Robin* D. Stone sites the research conducted by David Finkelhor *A Source Book on Child Sexual Abuse,* who describes the four major ways in which abuse causes lifelong problems for survivors.

1. Stigmatization—Guilt, shame, and self-blame; could lead survivors to feel bad about them selves and hurt themselves.
2. Powerlessness—Instability to stop the abuse; could lead to passivity, lashing out, or controlling behavior.
3. Betrayal—Loss of trust and grief over loss of the relationship, especially when the abuser is related; could lead to difficulty trusting others.
4. Traumatic Sexualization—Distress, confusion and painful or inappropriate sexual experience; could lead to obsessive or fear about sex.

Reaction to the Trauma of rape

1. Loss of appetite
2. Nausea and/or stomach aches
3. Headaches

4. Loss of memory and/or concentration
5. Change in sleep pattern

Psychological and Emotional reaction

1. Denial and/or guilt
2. Shame or humiliation
3. Fear and feeling of loss and control
4. Loss of self respect
5. Anger and anxiety
6. Nervous or compulsive behavior
7. Depression and mood swings
8. Withdrawal from relationships
9. Changes in sexual activity

In Reading *Beginning to Heal* I found the authors made a rather interesting suggestion, which can help all survivors of abuse, get over the abuse or challenge their energies in a positive direction.

1. Don't try to hurt or kill yourself.
2. Remind yourself that you're not going crazy.
3. Find people you can talk to.
4. Allow yourself to think about the abuse as much as you need to. Drop any responsibilities that aren't essential.
5. Don't use alcohol or drugs to stop the pain.
6. Get out of dangerous or abusive situations.
7. Sit tight and ride out the storm.
8. Develop a belief in something greater than yourself.
9. Talk to people who are farther along in their healing.

10. Do as many things for yourself as possible.

Often time's children and adults alike go to great lengths to deny their own perception of an abuse.

Dwight
Age: 20

"When my step father would come in my room at nights; I would imagine that it was all a dream, that he was a monster. I would close my eyes tight when the penetration started, wanting to cry and hoping it will end and when morning comes I will forget it".

One of the most common ways abusers deal with hurt is denial. We try to pretend that it never happened. But to heal, we have to face the truth.

Duane
Age: 27

"Even after he forced his penis inside of me and I went to bed that night bleeding, I never knew it was rape.
Even when he was my lover for two years I still never considering it to be rape".

Most children and adult victims of abuse blame themselves, as they believe that it was their fault. Some men feel guilt, as they were unable to protect themselves. But what you need to do understand is that sexual abuse is *never* the fault of the child. Some victims of abuse feel pain and anguish while others find pleasure. If the abuse felt good, you may have felt ashamed and think that you wanted it to happen. It is natural to have sexual feelings when you're touched in a sexual manner. The child or young man who when sexually abused may have an erection or even ejaculate, but that does not mean that they wanted it.

Paul
Age: 32

"I was only fourteen when he fuck me from behind, it was rough and painful. Today I only find pleasure from rough sex, was that because of the rape?"

I have taken a few notes from Robin D. Stone *"No Secrets No Lies: How Black Families Can Heal From Sexual Abuse"* she notes that there are other forms of therapies available to get over the pain. She argues that "for some of us, talking about our problems is not enough" and for me it isn't. In other cases it's just not the best way we can express ourselves. The ultimate goal she argues is to "acknowledge that trauma happened and has affected you and then release it and move on". Stone quotes Turner, Melinda, a social Worker with a managed-care company in San Francisco. Alternative therapies are particularly helpful when dealing with incidents that happened when you were young and couldn't even articulate or understand what was happening. Turner also recommended that creative expression could be therapeutic. I find this to be very true as sometimes it is difficult to verbally explain what happened to you and sometimes you just can't find the words to express yourself.

I took the writing suggestion from my doctor and it helped and I have not stopped writing up to this day, as it eases my mind. Nothing is wrong with keeping journals as men; it's perfectly healthy to keep a written reflection of your thoughts and experiences. I know of a few men who have being sexually abused and they are excellent writers today. Getting in tuned with your creative side is one great means of self-help. I have now develop a greater love for all types of music, from classical to jazz and Rhythm and blues, to reggae to dancehall and lots more. It's the aesthetic feel that music gives to me that gives me the strength to move on most days. Nina Simone "Nobody knows you when you're down and out", "I want a little sugar in my bone" and *Ne Me Quitte Pas* bring chills to my spine whenever I listen to them and I feel at times as if she was singing just for me. At times when I get depressed or lonely, music is all that can comfort me, it takes me to a place that relaxes my mind or even allow me to cry as I feel each note that the singer sings. I feel the joys and sadness deep within the songs, each time I listen to Mary J. Blige *No more Drama* I cry as I am convinced she wrote it just for me. My life would not be the same without singers like Janet Jackson, Brandy, Monica, Usher, Tevin Campbell, Bob Marley, Patti Label, Whitney Houston, Brandy, Maria Cary, and Tina Turner to name a few. Tina turner once said that "Music saves" and it surely does help to ease depression.

Seeking help and getting the anger out isn't easy, but in order to heal, it is important that we start talking. The more we talk about the abuse the easier it is for us as victims to come to term that it happened. I have survived and lived to talk about it so that others may not have to go through what I had to endure for years.

It takes a conscious decision from each individual victim to come to terms with their past, face the past and attempt at dealing with it. I would be naive to want to suggest to survivors of sexual abuse in Jamaica that it is easy to get over the anger, the pain and depression. It is even harder finding someone to talk to, but we have to take a chance, only then can we know the truth. At the end of the book, I have listed resources and related books that deal with sexual abuse that I have read or have been suggested to me. I can lead the horse to the water but I can't force the horse to drink of the water. Change comes only from within.

My greatest challenge in writing was to get the stories of other men. While I have interviewed over 300, some just never wanted to have their story in my book and others I just never felt comfortable with their story. There is a deeper meaning behind the title as crying for me means strength and I wanted the stories of those men who have overcome rape and sexual abuse or those who have not over abused themselves and not in denial. I strongly believe that when a man cries he is letting out his anger in a positive light as without crying he may use that pain and anger in a negative way and may be end up in jail as most black men. It's a cycle and it takes only one to stop and break it. I wanted these guys to give me their stories in their own words, some have while I had to write others stories as they just could not find the right words. Well I understand as I found the same problem myself. I thank all those who have shared their stories with me even though they are not recorded in this book but thanks nonetheless. Here is the story of a young boy, his story reminded me of mine so much and I just had to tell it.

Tye 38
Location: Jamaica
Occupation: Teacher

It was a rainy evening and it seemed as if the rain would never end and there was lighting and thunder and I was a bit scared. O'Neal one of my very close friends and my neighbor was away at church camp and I was spending the day at his house playing video games. Jermain, O'Neal's brother and I were friends and I usually hang out with him even when O'Neal was not home. He was a typical girl's man and I look up to him and at one point wanted to be just like him. He used to play football for his school and he was a star player. He invited me into his room that rainy evening, I enjoyed going in his rooms as he had pictures of women on his walls and he had a collection of porn magazines that I love to look at.

I was fascinated by the pictures of naked women I was 14 years old and I was never sexually active yet. Jermain gave me a copy of a Playboy and a Hustler magazine and each morning before I go to school I would look at the picture of this sexy ass blond girl and jerk off. I had got close to sex but was a bit scared that I could not perform well enough so I usually back off. Jermain loves to talk about sex and often times he would laugh at me for been a virgin. That night I was laying in his bed looking at porn and I had an erection as always which was visible to Jermain and he asked me what that was. In a jovial way he touched me and I pushed his hands away. I felt a bit uncomfortable by the touch but hey it was Jermain, he was a girls man I trusted him. He wanted to compare penis size as he said that the bigger the penis the greater the sex. I wasn't interested but he showed me his and I laughed at him as mine was much bigger. I decided out of fun and laugher to show him mine and then he began to wrestle with me.

While the wrestling was playful it went out of hand. We were rubbing our bodies against each other and it felt great, honestly it did. He was much stronger than I was and one thing led to another and Jermain f..ked me that night. It was a bit painful at first but he was gently and oddly enough I enjoyed it. It was a Friday night and I spent the night wrap in Jermain's arms. I was in a bit of pain but just seeing Jermain's next to me in bed made me feel special. Jermain was 27 years old at the time and he was the football coach for the local high school. The sex continued for four years and I never saw myself, as been a homosexual.

Jermain was a part of my life, the first time I had sex with a girl I had it in his room. He even encouraged me to engage in oral sex with a woman. He was the best man at my wedding and even the godfather for my eldest son. We became best friends much closer than his younger brother. Even though I became a teacher and had a family of my own, I still enjoyed having sex with him. I still question my sexuality at age 38 but it's hard to find someone to talk to as they may not understand. It wasn't until I read this book on male sexuality and there was something that dealt with sexual abuse and how most victims of male sexual abuse never feel that they were abused, I then realized that Jermain abused me sexually. Its too late now, I am so old, what do I do? It's not easy talking about these things. Brain "I think you book is a lovely idea and I hope someone will read it and realize the truth and get help. I would love to get help, but I decide at this stage of my life I may loose my wife and kids and I don't think I can do that. I may never get help, but I hope my story will help someone."

Rory 25
Location:
California Occupation:

Hey wassup Brain?
I read the first chapter of your book online and I have to applaud you for taking up such a risky and culturally taboo subject. There are many boys that are molested and nobody hears about it, or do they have anyone to tell and sometimes they just need to know they are not the only one and that they can overcome the inner demons that comes with being molested.

I was molested at various periods in my childhood life and I have dealt with it, but prior to me dealing with it I had issues trusting people or even talking to people at all about anything, I was very shy so that I looked stupid, reclusive and some what antisocial also I was never able to have an ejaculation whenever I was with someone no matter how much stimulation I got. But over the past couple of years I have come to grips with it and have reconciled with God and everything is all good. So now I bear no shame about telling anyone that I was molested because it no longer has the grips on me that it did in the past. I'm glad you wrote this because victims of sexual abuse need to realize that they need to deal with the issues that came along with the abuse or they will forever live lives that are dysfunctional in one way or the other, some might be able to cover it up but deep down they know they have issues.
So far from the first chapter I can already identify with some of the things you went through but to varying degrees. But as you stated different people deal with it in different ways.

18

Sexual abuse and the family

○ ○
"My mother told me that I must have enjoyed it for it to happen the second time around with out saying anything to someone".

—O'Brien Dennis

A family member never molested me but the guy who first molested me knew my family and the man who raped me and later became my lover for two years knew my family also. The family unit is important in any child's life as family members are the first individuals they see and the first to socialize them and children develop a sense of trust for its members. In most cases when a child claims to be abused, the family never takes it seriously. Denial is one of the greatest forms of guilt a family can put on themselves about the truth of a situation. Craig is twenty-seven and lives in Tampa Florida with his new wife and child. He remembers the nights when his stepfather would come into his room and force him to have sex with him; he was only nine when it happened. Craig came from a typical middle class Jamaican family, they lived in Mandeville, his mother was a teacher and his stepfather worked with the local Bauxite Company.

After two years of sexual abuse, Craig started to become rebellious and one day after school he told his mother about what his stepfather was doing to him late in the nights. All he could remember was the sting of the belt she used to beat him for lying, lying at the man he had called father for six years and for also being ungrateful. He had a scar on his shoulders to remind him of that brutal beating his mother gave him. She knew what was going on, but she felt she had no choice and no control over the situation, as she could not support herself and three kids alone on a teacher's salary in Jamaica. She argued that he was well respected in the community and if he said anything to anyone she would kick him out of the house as it would bring about too much disgrace on the family. He not only had to face the resentment from his mother and her verbal abuse towards him, but he had to endure the continued sexual abuse by his stepfather. These were nights when he wanted to just die in his sleep, but he knew that his only escape was through education. After high school Craig got a scholarship for a school in the US and since college he has not returned to Jamaica and he no longer talk to his mother or any other family members.

The story is real and the circumstances surrounding the continued sexual abuse in Jamaica exist even today. Simple economics, mothers ignore the fact that their boys are being abuse by their men and because of economics, allow it to go on, it happen with girls more often than boys. I call it child prostitution at its best. I must note that the majority of wealth in Jamaica is owned by five percent of the population and that more than forty percent of Jamaicans live in abject poverty. It's all about survival and mothers are willing to make sacrifices to save their families, how sad? There are cases were women are uneducated and have three children with mouths to feed and her only means of support is a man. He physically abuses her and she is aware of the abuse of her child but because of survival, she keeps her moth shut, hoping that it will end soon and that she will find away out for her kids soon enough. In most case women find it hard to find a solution and yet another boy is confused and has lost all hope.

Sexual abuse of boys within Jamaican communities are hardly heard of or not reported out of shame. Boys are taught from early to be strong men, independent and in some cases forced to become the head of the family as in most cases there exist no father. The absence of father within the Jamaican social context dates back to slavery, as planters never encouraged families. It was one way to keep his "flock" submissive and obedient to him only. Separate and apart from "breeder" going around to rape women to get them pregnant to increase the slave population, the masters were busy raping young black boys and nothing was said, it was never spoken about because it was "massah' who did it. It is so sad that some bad qualities of our masters have been handed down to our men and yet slavery has ended. it is no surprise that sexual abuse of boys are common, underreported, unrecognized and under treated. Some boys would want to speak up, but in a society were homophobia is a Phenomenon young boys live each day hearing the open condemnation of homosexuality. No one will ever want to speak up but someone must and will break the cycle and I have done it and you can also. My mother rang into my head as a child that if she ever found out that I am gay "she would get a gunman kill me". This is common among most Jamaican households. I like most boys who were sexually abused, constantly questioned our sexual orientation and our masculinity.

Richard Gartner in an article titled "*About Male Sexual Victimization*" argues that 'the shame that accompanies such doubts silence many boys about their experiences. Yet if abuses remain unacknowledged and untreated, it may lead to such personal and societal consequences as depression, anxiety and other mental health problems, in addition to self-destructive behaviors, substance abuse and family destruction.

Robin Stone argues that child sexual abuse is like a ripple effect as ultimately it will affect each family member and her arguments also supports those presented by Gartner's theory on mental health problems if adults refuse to respond to the issue of sexual abuse in one way or another. I grew up with the constant fear that my younger sister may one day become sexually abused and I fear that I may not be able to protect her. I have sat her down and talk to her and I have even explained to her what rape is and she got scared and cried but she needs to know reality. I have taught her to love her body as a temple, her gift from God and no man should touch her in any shape or form. As a brother, as a survivor I have given her the strength to want to have the courage to speak up when she is touched in a sexual manner by anyone. I love her too much to want her to go through what I have been through.

My older sister and mother have dealt with the abuse in much the same way as the rest of the family. It has been over two years since my sister know and close to a year since I have told my mother and I am yet to get a hug or a comforting word. My family only concern is to keep it as a secret, they will be all shocked when the book is out but I have forgiven them. It is no secret within the family by now about what happen to me, but I am considered a grown man and as a man I should deal with the trauma of my rape and abuse as such, in silence and denial. It is a secret that no one wants to talk about it's as if it had never happened. Its upsetting how at the way they have dealt with it, some member of the family no longer acknowledge that I even exist and the fact that I have engaged in homosexual practices have some what allowed some members to cut off communication with me completely. It isn't about me, I thought I was the victim but its as if my family were hurt more than I have, but I have survived and that is all that matters.

I can imagine that it is more difficult for boys who have been abused by a family member to cope with dealing with the family. Robin Stone argues "in the case of abuse between adolescent or children, parents may find themselves torn between loyalty to a child who is the abusers and loyalty to the survivor". It is not easy on the family and even though it is harder for the victims to cope, it is hard to shut off a love one for such an act. A mother's love for a child is endless, so when a sibling abuses another, the mothers love is torn and when her husband is the abuser, she is forced to love him unconditionally no matter what he does, as she made that pledge before God.

My home country is still relatively poor, and while a vibrant extended family system exist, it fosters sexual abuse among family members. The family unit is close knit and in most cases over three generations sometimes reside under one roof, sleeping space is limited and younger and older children are forced to share beds. I remember meeting Ron two years ago on 14th street in Manhattan, he had mistaken me for a friend of his, but we only had facial similarities. We automatically developed a conversation and some what told him about my idea of writing a book about sexual abuse of young boys in Jamaica. He was eager to hear why I was interested in such a topic, and it was more interesting to hear his story. We have now lost touch but it brought pain to my eyes when he told me that his older cousin molested him. He told me that he lived in one of Kingston poor inner cities and his family lived in a two-bedroom house. A gunman shot his aunt and his mother took in her three children and along with her two made it five kids in the house. He said, they never had much privacy in the house but many a nights he could not only hear his mother having sex but he could also see her as all that separated her room from theirs was a thin curtain.

As sad as it may sound, he said he was about fourteen and he found himself being aroused sexually whenever he heard his mother and one night he caught his cousin in the dark masturbating to the sexual sounds of his mother. Ron explained that at fourteen he had not had sex with girls yet as he was a bit shy, and he was curious about his cousin masturbating so he would watch him from a distance. He was caught masturbating one night and his cousin encouraged him to continue. One thing led to another and his cousin started to fondle him and over a period of time he started to penetrate him. It only happened in the dark, so they could hardly see each other or each other's emotion. For the cousin it was just sex, he was only sixteen years old. His cousin died at seventeen by a stray bullet but Ron argues that even though he disliked the sensation he looked up to his cousin and had the utmost respect for him. In all shapes or form, this is a common case of sexual abuse and not child's play or innocent experimentation. It was soothing relaying each other's story as strangers as we both had things in common.

Sexual abuse of boys occurs quite often in Jamaica and in most cases families never talk about it. We need to educate our children more and talk to them about sex. Parents still refuse to discus sex as it is considered a taboo topic. My mother never gave me sex education, I learnt about sex by experimenting. It is important to note that sexual abuse of boys within the Jamaican social context is not a poor thing, it happens across all social section, poor and rich and it has no religious or color barrier. What parents need to do is talk, talk and do more talking. Stop forcing your boys to be men before time, give them the time and the space to experience their childhood innocence and enjoy their adolescent years.

The sexual abuse of boys although perceived by many black families as taboo is dangerous, but what is more dangerous is the denial that incest or sexual abuse of boys occur. In *Don't Tell: The Sexual Abuse of Boys*, Michel Dorois, talks about intergenerational and interfamilial abuse, which is the abuse between brothers or between cousins? These are practices, which without a doubt happen more frequent than we believe. Sexual aggression at times starts from within the home, with aggression going after the younger brother.

During one of my many visits to my second home at my father in Sunderland, I met a young man in the www.go-Jamaica.com chat room while I was doing research at the W.E.B. Du Bois Library on the UMASS campus in Massachusetts. The young man lived in Boston and he was twenty-one years old, and attends a local community college. He moved to the United States at age nineteen in search of a better life. He is not gay, however he is curious about the gay lifestyle. He currently resides with his aunt and uncle who forbid him from going out much as they profess to be Christians. As always I found some creative means to introduce the subject of my book as I was always looking for new case study. To my surprise after telling the young man some of the stories I had thus far, he told me quite openly and candidly about being sexually abused by both his male cousin and his brother.

Due to financial constrains I was unable to meet this young man in person, but we kept the communication via the telephone. We have now both lost contact as I had lost my mobile, however I was able to get him to trust me to the point where he was able to open up to me and tell me his horrific tale of incest. He said he was about eight when it all started and escalated more during his pubescent years. He said that he looked more mature for his age, had a thick built and was physically mature for his age. He asserted that both his brother and cousin would perform oral sex on him and on several occasions forced him to penetrate them. This happened until age nineteen when he left Jamaica. He does not consider himself gay even though he has engaged in homosexual acts. He wants to be with a woman but each time he gets close to intimacy he gets scared and feels that he would not perform. He is confused, and it is so sad that the information I have currently I never had it then so that I could relay it to him. This book is also dedicated to him. He has never told any member of his family and strongly believes that no one would believe him and the fact that the family are Christians, all they would do is keep it a secret and pray about it. I can not even stress how important family is and how important it is for families to deal with these issues and fess up to the reality of abuse, as in the end, it will do more harm than good if we deny the reality of incest and sexual abuse.

19

Why do we trust?

"Another day will find me brave, And not afraid to dare."

—*Clarissa Scott Delaney*

By the time I was twenty I had reintroduced my father into my life and I had gained a precious gift, a gift that I have prayed for years and that was a brother. We are just a year apart and he has the name of my then best friend. The day I met my father for the first time was one of the strangest feelings I could remember in my life. We had corresponded for a while, but I decided to visit him at his home in the US. He never met my expectations of the father I had wanted, but it gave me a sense of pride that I was finally seeing the man who helped to create me. He was slim, tall, well-toned, almond shade, muscles, bald, with a thick beard. I am a reflection of him in his youthful days and just as how he was proud to see me after all these years I was proud to see him, my father for the first time in my life. Seeing my father took away a lot of hurt and anger from my heart, and even though I never hated him, I was upset with him for not being there. For some strange reason, I felt that if he was around he could have protected me, but it was all in my past. To this day I have not accepted an apology, even though he has offered to give me one, the most important thing is that he is now willing to be a father and that is all that matters. The one thing that I respect my mother for the most and that is, while I was growing up she never said bad things about my father or discouraged me from loving him. She always said the best things about him and reminded me constantly that no matter what the differences between them; he was still and will always be my father. I grew up loving the father I never knew and when I met him for the first time at age twenty, I never wanted an explanation for why he was never a part of my life, I was just happy that he was now ready to own up to the responsibility that I was his child. I do feel hurt at times, as I felt that he neglected me all these years because he never wanted me and I sometimes used to blame him for my abuse, as if I had a male figure in my life, maybe I would have known how to defend myself and be more of a man.

That night when I arrived at his house, it was late, about after 2am and my brother who had traveled with my father to pick me up in New York, who never spoke a word to me for the three and a half hours journey, took me in his arms that early morning and took a picture of both of us. It was more than a Kodak moment as it meant a lot to me, to know that I was accepted. That summer was one of my best summers in my life. My dad got me a job at a local lumberyard. The physical work was tiresome but in the end it gave me some well needed muscles and I never had this weak feeble look to me anymore. I spent a lot of time with my brother getting to know him some more and giving him the chance to know me. We have so much in common. Being the rebellious child I was then I felt that by piercing my ears I would attract more girls, remember at this point in my life I still did not consider myself gay, so I did, my father was pissed but I never gave a f——k. I was re-introduced to AOL that summer and while searching through the chat rooms, I realized that the life I lived, my fears, my struggles and dreams were not unique to me, I was not alone. Young men, my age, younger and older, lived my fear and pain and there were a few who were comfortable with who they are and the men they had become.

I returned to Jamaica with a new attitude, a new man, I now dressed well, looked well, I was more confident and I now had the strength to go get help. My brother introduced me to www.go-jamaica.com/chat a Jamaican chat site and there I found young men on campuses that were questioning themselves and I gradually developed a new set of friends. It was as if the sun shone on me alone whenever I walked, as I walk with grace and poise. I felt accepted in the world that once neglected me. I now realized that I was not sick, my thoughts and feelings were real, and just like me, there were so many others, who wanted to be heard, and who wanted to be free, but the world we lived in we had to hide if we were to be the men we wanted. I would spend endless nights in the computer lab talking in the chat room, and most of my days were spent in the library. No one knew what I was doing, it would be odd sometimes, but I met in that chat room, many times, classmates, who were in the computer lab next to me and we discovered ourselves right there in the library. I was scared of having sex, but I was curious to know how they were coping with their sexuality and I was curious to know, if any one of them got raped just like I had. The discovery was alarming. Many of them and I write with pain and anger, many were molested by family, relatives or family friends.

There were nights I would go back to my room, crying asking God why did he allow these men to do these horrible things to these young men. We were bright, intelligent and we had a future, why f…k that all up and bring about all this confusion. I was embarrassed at one point to tell anyone or even admit to myself that after a while, I began to enjoy the sex with my rapist and that he became my first love. Its true, but this was how sex was introduced to me and so many others like myself, and nothing is wrong in saying that we enjoyed it. Now who could say that oral stimulation was never a great feeling, sure, we were introduced to sex by men, men who themselves may have been molested, but the act was wrong. These adults have a responsibility to protect children and not to take advantage of us in the ways they did. It was the story of the young man, who lived on my block, Taylor Hall, who was raped by his brother and at twenty-two years old, continues to have sex with his brother. He loves his brother so much, that he could never see himself stop giving his brother pleasure.

Within less than five months, I had corresponded with more than fifty men some on campus some off campus that were as confused as I was. I had developed a sense of trust for many of them. I was caught up with school and was unable to meet with most of these guys but to this day I have some of them on my MSN chat buddy list. I had only two months before my finals and I was busy completing my final year research paper. It was a most stressful time, I never had enough money to complete the paper and my mid term grades weren't the best and so it was making me somewhat depressed. I was also caught up with trying to find a job after school so that I would never just walk out of University without a direction of where my life was going to turn.

I had spent the winter of 2001 in New York and in Massachusetts; most of my time was spent indoors and with nothing to do I concentrated more on my physical built as I was now into my appearance and what the world around me thought about me. I did a bit of shopping in New York and got a pretty good number of leftover summer clothes from H&M in both states. I was well toned and I now had muscles. I started wearing muscle shirts, tight jeans and sandals, the typical rude boy Jamaican look. I would have to take you the reader to see for yourself how a rude boy Jamaican youth flex, he has a typical gay look, and might I say acts feminine, and yet in a culture that pervades homophobia such behaviors are acceptable. There were a few guys who were after me but honestly I was not interested in engaging myself in any form of homosexual activity until I had completed my degree. Honestly, I knew that my feelings towards men would get stronger as time went by, but I was not ready to be rushed into it. I was not ready mentally to deal with that aspect of my life. In my mind I wanted to get my degree get a job, find a woman and get married and live happily ever after. The gay side of me I wanted to explore long after I had children and established a marriage. I would go on dates, just to talk and relax my mind and these were on campus. I refused to have sex, not that I was shy about it, but emotionally my mind was not there yet.

I met this one young man, Andy he was 16 years old when we first met and he attended a prominent high school in Kingston. He was fun to be around, we would talk for hours and strangely enough despite his age he taught me a lot about the gay life out there. He lived with his grandmother. Although someone took care of her so he had all the free time in the world. He was a rather intelligent young man who had a great future ahead of him. He was head of the debating society, a prefect and he was planning on going to Europe that summer in search of schools. Of all the men that I came across, he was the only person that if I had decided to have sex with it would have been with him. I never did however as in my mind he was too young and I felt that he was probably more confused than I was, but trust me he wasn't. We had seen each other naked as he would visit me many times on campus. I was scared most of the times and I would lock him up in my room. Though I never took the chance to sleep with him, grown men slept with him and gave him lots of money. He had a feminine vibes to him, and he was not ashamed of who he was. I wasn't ready for all that yet. He would call names, but for legal reasons, I choose not to make mention of any of those men as Jamaicans who read this book would say I was lying. Trust me, he wasn't lying but I never saw him doing it so I can't say for sure that it is the truth. But I have seen some prominent men around him and it's so sick that they could take advantage of such a young child.

Most of my free time was spent talking to Andy chatting online and consuming myself with school. There was a young man I fancied online, we had not met in person, only spoke on the phone and he was very interesting. We would talk before he went to work each morning and we would send each other to bed most nights. I wanted to meet up with him but time just never permitted and each time I decided to, something came up and I had to cancel. I had not seen this young man physically and thus had no sexual desires for him and it was mutual between the both of us, it was just mutual friendship. He was twenty-four years old and I would encourage him to get a first degree and make himself more marketable. It was such an odd feeling but most days while in a lecture or in the library I would think of him, I never saw a picture of him before but based on his personality I painted a face and a body in my mind. The long distance friendship evolved into both of us trusting each other; well that was how I felt then. I would tell him about my problems with my mother and how I felt she never had my interest at heart and he would talk to me about how much he was trying to suppress his gay desires. I would encourage him to go to church and pray to God about it but I knew that within itself was easier said than done. His family was a bit suspicious of him as he had no girlfriend and he was not the typical young Jamaican man, he never had a child yet and that is one give away in Jamaica. The notion of being fruitful and multiply is culturally embedded in the minds of Young men. We met online in January of 2001. He would profess his love for me but how could I love someone I never knew before. He made me feel wanted, that much I knew and he always took the time to listen to me and he never beat me down, he was a pillar of support.

Two weeks leading up to the end of classes and the start of finals April 2001, I had decided to meet with him. I knew after exams that I would leave Kingston and take a long needed break in the countryside where I was from. It was a difficult two weeks as there were constant power outages across the island. Each time we were to meet, the electricity would be off, while we had lights on campus he never felt comfortable meeting me on my building. My place of residence was renowned for gay bashing. The last weekend of April 2001, was my last chance to meet with him, and even though there was a blackout that night I still decided to take a chance and have dinner with him. I had developed a sense of trust for this guy and felt it was just an innocent date. He asked if he could take a friend and as it was just dinner I figured the more the merrier, I was to later find out that they both wanted to be too merry.

His friend was in his mid forties, he looked a bit old for his age but hey I was not interested in him. He had a wife and three grown children but they all resided in the United States, but he felt more comfortable residing in Jamaica where he could mess around with poor young boys. It was a Saturday night and we drove in Michael's friend's car to a Japanese restaurant in New Kingston. I can still remember that night so vividly as if it was yesterday. Although there was a blackout, New Kingston was lit by generators and though the streets were not busy with people, it was visible with people who were mainly looking for food to buy. I had always enjoyed the New Kingston strip, most Mondays I would visit the Jamaica Tourist Board and later have lunch at Burger King across from Citi Bank. The restaurant we went to was located across from the Jamaica Tourist Board's Kingston office, close to a police station that was behind the Hilton Kingston hotel. The Asylum nightclub was a few doors down from the restaurant I think. Jamrock Sports Bar and Grill was not far either, it was notorious for its gay patrons and I was always scared to go inside. The word *"sport"* is actually a pun as it refers to homosexuals in Jamaica; this was information I gathered while living in the US. There were lights in the restaurant but Kingston was in darkness. I remember Buju Banton *"Kingston hot hot hot"* playing on the radio. The restaurant was a bit crowded and Michael suggested that we go to his friend's house, as he had electricity there and we would be more comfortable. I never wanted to remain in the crowded restaurant so I decided that it was a good idea. Remember, I don't know these two men that well; I had just developed a bond with Michael over the phone, that was all.

We arrived at the house, which was somewhere off Norman Manley Boulevard. The older guy's house was quite homely; it reminded me more of my home back in the country. We all sat in the living room and ate, Michael was aquatinted with the house and so I had asked him for some water, as I had not bought anything to drink. We were watching BET and being a young man I was in tuned to popular culture. I realized that Michael had disappeared but I never thought much of it. I started developing a conversation with his friend and one conversation led to another until he started talking about sex. I told him that I was not gay yet and I was NOT enthused in having gay sex anytime soon. He told me that Michael had informed him that I had a huge penis, which was a lie and I objected to such accusations. He later told me that a man with my frame should have a big "tool" as he is tall and has over ten inches of hard muscle. That was information I never really wanted to hear. He touched me on a few occasions and he got a bit upset when I turned down his advances.

While this rass old man was trying to look mi, Michael was in a room all by himself, mi later find him a feel up him buddy, mi walk out a the room as I was not interested in what he was doing. A couple a seconds after mi walk out him come in a the passage way half-naked and ask me wa meck mi walk out. Mi tell him say mi never did come fi fuck or play wid no man buddy, all mi did come fi do was to see him in person and chat some more. Him tell mi say a lie mi did a tell. The bwoy did look good, sexy no rass and ah was a bit curious cause him buddy did look good too. I was just uncomfortable with this rass old man up in a mi face. Michael went back inside of the room and the old man walk in behind him, and stupid mi, ah go inside bout fifteen minutes as mi did want fi know wa them did a do inside. Yes, mi did fuck man before and "Him" did fuck mi too, but after age 16 mi never go wid another man and futher more, mi was nat a batty man. Mi did always want fi see two man fuck so out a curiosity mi go in a the room.

When mi go in a di room, them did both naked as the day them did barn and them did a play with each other buddy. Them never did a suck it or anything, them just did a play, the old man, buddy did BIG no rass, bout 11inches and it was the first mi ever see buddy so big. Sure mi cocky did get hard after seeing all that. Mi never did want to join and mi never did a look fi fuck or get fuck, and that is the plain truth. Michael was cute and mi did feel something bout him that mi did like and even though mi would a consider messing around with him, I was not in the mood, I was more thinking about mi exams them on Monday. A part of mi did want fi do something but mi did just hate the idea of this old man in mi space. May be if it was Michael alone in a di house we would a fuck.

Michael tell me to come over but mi tell him no. By this time mi pants was at mi ankle and the two of them could a see mi stiff cocky. Mi still never did feel comfortable wid the old man and further more him buddy did too big and mi never did want fi encourage him. Eventually the old man was there sucking Michael's buddy and though ah did like the smile pan Michael's face mi never want the old man touch mi. All mi do was to just stand in a di corner an all mi do was to play with mi cocky and ah was quite comfortable doing that by mi self. What mi was doing was ok and the night was going to end soon and mi would just call it a night.

The older man look up pan me with Michael's buddy in a him mouth and ask mi who a go fuck who, and mi meck it clear to them both say mi nah go fuck nor get fuck tonight. All of a sudden the man jump off a di bed and push me. Although mi was upset mi did a keep mi cool, him drag mi over to the bed, then me realize say him serious no rass now. Where was Michael in all this? While the man had push mi, he had walked out of the room. The old man hold mi hands them across the bed and tell mi say a bwoy like me can teck buddy good as mi slim and have the right bady. Stupid me, mi did think say fi some odd reason him just did a scare me, but no, him did serious. Mi now start fi fight him off, and tell him bout him bloodclath and start fi call out fi Michael, but him nevea answer. All mi push and turn, this rass old man did too strong fi mi. Him was about 6'4' and about 200lbs. Now mi did start fi cry, cause mi no longer had control over mi body and mi did feel like say mi a loose mi breath.

This man was old enough to be my grandfather and here him was on top of me, and I had no clue what him was about to do. Him turn mi face down on the bed and him drag down mi pants, him never touch mi shirt, mi did teck off mi shoes at the door. Him hold on to mi wrist and hold out mi two hand them an him use him knee and pin mi now in a mi knee them from back way. It did a hurt mi no rass, but no matta wa mi do, this rass man woulda neva ease up aff a mi. Mi was weak, mi body did feel lifeless, at one point mi did try fi cry but no words never come from mi mouth. All mi did want fi do was just die, teck a nife and stab miself.

Mi never give up the fight, cause mi say mi never did want no buddy. Michael came back into the room and I felt that he would put a stop to all this rass madness, but him too started to hold me down. The old man move up futher on top a me and Michael hold mi legs them open from behind. Mi feel him hand them open up mi batty cheeks and then mi feel this cool wet thing him put in a mi batty. A wish to rass, God could a come fi him earth now, a would a zap myself to hell if mi was a obeah man, mi would a sell mi soul to the devil, just not to get fuck. Mi cry out even more, but who the fuck was in the house to hear me, no bady. At one point mi cry out so loud mi never hear a sound come out a mi voice. God!! what the rass was I sopose to do? It was my fault, no bady never did tell mi fi come a this rass man yard and further more no bady never did force me to come either.

As Michael open up mi legs, and try fi put him buddy inside a mi, mi try fi fight them off still, mi twis mi bady, back and forth, but them hold me even harder. Trust mi, mi did fraid a buddy as Michael was big, almost like me and seen that it was a long time since I had sex back there, ah knew it was going to hurt like fuck. Michael got on top of mi now and put him knees in a mi leg them and force him big buddy in a mi batty. Mi scream out fi mercy, mi push and mi turn but nothing I did could have prevent Michael from putting him buddy inside a mi. It was like using a sharp knife to cut open a coconut an you have fi force the knife in fi cut the coconut as the outside shell hard. A so mi did feel, mi batty did tight an him force him way inside a mi, it was as if him did a push up everything mi did eat the night back up inside a mi belly.

The room that we was in did big, and the night air out side did dead, you could a hear a pin if it did drop when we first enter the house. The color of the paint on the wall was cream or off white and the light from the bed side table created a reflection on the wall. There was an air conditioner in the room and it was on, so the room did feel a bit cool. The curtains on the wall was floral, like some pice a clath material you granmada use to wear in a the country, prity no rass, a beez could a meck a nest pan it. The sheet pan the bed was the same print as the curtain on the walls and the bed was big, more like a queen size bed.

Honestly mi did try fi fight them both off, mi scream, kick, but it was no help. I was laying cross way in the bed, and the old man was now standing holding my hands and Michael pound him buddy inside a me. Mi could a hear the moaning sound the nasty old man did a meck as him watch Michael as him fuck mi. Michael, never teck him time, no, him did a try fi get me relax but mi couldn't. The way it did feel was as if him did a put him hand in a dry dirt fi drill a hole and it couldn't go in as the dirt was too dry, that was how it felt.

Mi did a feel the same burning sensation me did feel at 14 when di man mi did call the love of mi life, and then mi feel all the anger and rage mi had when mi did go home the night and see the blood. This night was no different, cause mi did ago bleed. Mi did try fi fight him off even more as it did a pain the hell out a mi. Mi then decide fi close mi eyes as it had to end, him had to cum. Mi lack mi eye tight and think bout jumping off Rick's Café' in Negril, something that mi never ever think about, but it felt dangerous and mi think say the fall alone would kill mi. Mi did also remember the sun set, with all the colors the sun use to set, when them white people use to go to Rick's just for the view of the sunset. It meck you mind feel at ease just looking at the sun going down unda the sea, it was as if you were in heaven and God was calling you to bed. Mi did have to get mi mind relax cause mi did learn say its betta fi relax than tense up cause then it would a hurt u more. Mi pray to God that Michael would come quick, mi tell God a quick prayer and tell him say mi ago start go back a church every Saturday and mi did ago get baptize if him save mi from this one. Is only in time of trouble we sometimes talk to God. This was more than talking me did a reason one on one with God as only him alone could save me.

Michael's force was getting stronga and mi could a feel him a hit a wall inside a mi belly bottom and it hurt like when u teck a sharp knife a cut a bwoy and all u see is white flesh and no blood. Mi know when him did a come, as him start fi breath heavy and push him buddy in a mi futher and futher. Him grab on to mi tight tight when him did a cum and scream out, fuck, fuck!! And then fall on top a mi like some dead rass man.

Even though him cum inside a me, him did have on a condom, and although it never matta, at lease mi never did have fi worry bout STD or HIV as mi did get enough knowledge about sex and how to protect mi self. When him get up off mi and pull it out mi hear a pop sound like when u pop a cork at new years ever ball and that was it. Mi lay down in a di bed, pan mi bell an mi feel all kind a things in a mi bady and in a mi head. By that time the old man was no where to be found and Michael was now standing before me, asking me if mi all right. Mi tell him say fi move him little pussy hole before mi cause him just rape me. Him tell mi say a joke me a joke. Even though mi eyes them did red, him say a so man fi get fuck, and mi could a teck a buddy good and him want some more. Me never had the strength to respond nor the strength to get up. Finally mi get up and wipe myself up and tell them say fi call mi a cab. Mi never have enough money but mi was going to take a chance. Stupid me! Michael tell mi say that was all taken care off, cause the caby was outside a wait pan me. Then and then mi realize say it was all a set up.

When mi go outside mi say mi did ago go to the police but Babylon never did ago believe me, them did ago beat me rass, laugh after me and tell the world say mi a batty boy. The only gunman mi did know did dead so mi couldn't get mi bwoy them kill him, so mi was on mi own once more. No bady fi talk to and no where to go. I had convinced myself that by the time mi go back on campus mi did ago hang myself. The driva never say a word to me, it was obvious that him did come pan them mission ya before and him did know the runnings. Him just ask mi if mi cool and where him did fi drop mi off. Mi tell him campus and tell him say when mi reach mi will meck mi fren them pay him, but him say it was all covered. Mi did want fi cry even more, but mi never did want him fi see mi like that. Him drive me back to campus in dead silence, all I was hearing was Muta Baruka on the radio talking shit as always bout the white man and him slavery bull shit.

The hardest part of the night was yet to come and that was walking on Taylor Hall, seeing people that I knew I went to class with and wanting to say, I am hurting and I need to go to the doctor, but the words could not come. I just wanted to lie down, cry, and I was convinced that I was going to jump from the third floor of my dorm. When I reached my door to my surprise a group of friends were sitting at my door waiting on me. I never wanted to sit and talk but Natania insisted that I sit and chat. I refused and she dragged me down on the cold hard bench that was at my door and can you imagine how my ass hurt even more then. My eyes were red, I remember Natania asking why my eyes were so red, if I was smoking weed and I told her that it was the stress of the exams pressure. That night I knew how truly strong I was as I tried to clear my mind and enjoy the company of friends. I sat on that hard bench for over four hours and when I finally decided to go inside my room, if only there was something to hang myself with I would be a dead man now. I had nothing else to live for, I knew I had to run, but run to where? I wanted so badly to talk to someone but who under Gods earth would believe me if I told them that I was raped by a man at age twenty-one?

The next day, which was a Sunday, I bought the Sunday paper, and I walked to the University Chapel, it's a lovely old church overlooking the administration building. That was the one place that caught my eyes when I first entered the gates of the University of the West Indies, Mona. I sat down under the aqueduct and it was as if my life was slowing passing me by. If I killed myself I would have wasted my life and I needed to find my place in life and in doing so, I would have to run away. I was not running away from my problems, I just wanted to re-new my spirit and I could no longer do it in Jamaica. I lay in the hot sun and I asked God to please let me pass my exams and get me out of this place. I confided in two friends that night and they laughed at me and told me that I wanted the dick and they claimed that out of fear of the guy talking, I decided to call it rape. Sure, many guys do that, but on this occasion, it was rape.

April 30, 2001

Jesus loves me this I know for the bible tells me so. Jesus I have not prayed in a long time, I have sinned and come short of the glory of God. Lord today I beg for your forgiveness, father my soul has been lost in the cold and my heart has now turned to stone. Father I don't know what to do or think anymore. Heaven gates are open wide and I am far a way from your gates, but lead me and guide me and

I will find a way. Father my eyes are filled with water, because I am all alone in a deep ocean. I beg for your mercy and guidance, amen.

What have I become or done to myself is not different from what the man who abuses drugs or alcohol. I have abused myself, trying to seek alternative to my problems. It was only a means to an end. I have hated myself for so long and what else could I have done nothing else. Sex for me was like taking a pill, easing the mother f__king pain, which was piercing through my soul. I am looking for a fucking answer. All of my friends have used me and taken advantage of me. I have been raped and molested. Who can I turn to when I need love? The answer is yet to be found.

I can still remember saying NO, stop motherfucker, I had to continue and bear the pain for it could get worst. It wasn't easy after he was finished, for I felt used and fucked up, yes I was but I felt as if my manhood was taken from me. I felt some motherfucking pain in my ass. I cried but what the fuck could I have done. I can only cry to myself, but until I have found someone who loves me for m, my life will remain the same.

My first exam was on Monday a day and a half after the rape and even though I could not concentrate I was convinced that the exam was easy and I could have passed it. It was Philosophy of Arts, it was easy and its common sense, I had to pass. A few months later I found out that I never did pass and it cost me my degree. I completed the degree in New York and that is all that matters now.

I never believed in failure and I made my point. I never regretted attending the University of the West Indies, what I regret most of all from my experience on campus is my levels of curiosity. If only I had walked away and never had a curious mind. Hey, I am not blaming myself but if only I had walk away from it all. Everything in life happens for a reason and God has a plan, his plan may have been for me to write this book and let it all out. God may have wanted me to open the gates and let other young men like my self know that they are not alone and that help is out there. It is never easy talking about abuse, as most times we think it was our fault and even though we might say its not, sometimes in the back of our minds we say that it is. When guys get raped it's a different ball game and I hope that each reader gets that point. None is greater than the other, but men find it much harder to heal and it's a much longer process.

At the end of writing this book, I still believe in trust and honesty, and I still visit strangers and nothing has happened to me. Many times, I meet a stranger and they offer to take me home and I go, out of trust and curiosity and sometimes it's the best decisions I have made in my life, I had gained long-term friendships from such encounters and today they mean the world to me. Life is all about risk and taking chances and being spontaneous. Many times my sporadic decisions have landed me jobs and I have met individuals who have touched my life in so many ways. I say to the readers, nothing is wrong with trusting a stranger, but use your instinct. Sometimes, something deep within us says don't go, as danger lies ahead, trust it, it may save your life. This has been a personal journey for me and I thank all my friends who have opened up their arms, pockets and homes to me over the past two and a half years. It was curiosity that brought us all together and it is trust that has kept us close for all these years and it will take us even further. At the end of the day (teary eyed) I could not have done it without all of you. I could call names but ya'll would kill me, but when I decided to start writing and leave the job and move from my apartment, I had enough keys to keep me warm for five winters.

My strength has been renewed and God has shown me the way. Good friends last forever and while a lover may last but only a few days, never turn your backs on your friends for when the nights get cold, they will keep you warm. These six months of writing has been great and writing was healing, it was a reflection on my life and where I want to be now. I have discovered that I hate water and that I am in love with pineapples and grape nut ice cream. I now realize the importance of music in my life, as Janet Jackson *Damita Jo* has kept me warm on the nights when I went to bed crying and needed someone next to me to keep me warm and safe. Brandy will always be my princess as too many days, her songs have kept me strong. The most important lesson of all is, I need help, I need to let the anger out, to cry, to weep, to let it all out. I honestly feel that before I had written this book I was trapped at age fourteen and at age twenty-one and I needed to let go. It took nights of endless crying and searching through my life to relive the memories and it was therapeutic and though I am not fully healed it was a lovely journey. In the end, I have one dream and that is to develop a non-profit organization for young men who have ran away from home and who need that extra push to complete their education. Special emphasis will be placed on black youth as the black community is yet to embraced sexual abuse of men. Many times we argue that black men don't want to go to school, but there are so many factors involved in preventing them from pursuing their goals. As I write, there are so many of my friends who need to complete school, but can't and for some who have told their parents that they are gay, they have turned their backs on them and they are left to fend for themselves. I feel for them, as when I ran away and came to this country, I got so much help and I would like to give back in some way or the other to those who are now in need now.

20

Forgiveness

○ ○

A Prayer of Humble Trust

Lord, I have given up my pride
and turned away from my arrogance
I am not concerned with great matters
or with subjects too difficult for me.
Instead, I am content and at peace.
As a child lies quietly in its mother's arms,
so my heart is quiet within me.
Israel, trust in the Lord Now and forever!
—Psalm 131

I never in my wildest dreams imagined that I could have run away from it all, but I did. I left Jamaica in such a rush, less than two months after the rape occurred. I had no clue where I was running. I just knew I had to go. To find myself. It had to be somewhere else other than home. I felt that what had happen to me was my fault. Curiosity kills the cat and it surely did kill my cat and now my soul was lost to the winds forever. I was yearning to regain it. Often at times I use to wonder why it had to take a horrible act as this to give Darrel a chance. A chance to open up my world to him. I hated Darrel. I hated him for not warning me about what could happen if I became too curious. I hated him for not being more persistent in his quest for me. I felt that at the time my self-worth was low. I felt then that I would have let anyone who wanted to f—-k me do so and I would not even care.

My life too no longer had any meaning for me. At that time I would have sold my soul to the devil for a dollar if he had asked me to. I wanted so badly to tell someone about what happened but I couldn't, I was too embarrassed. If I did, I would have had to explain how a grown man like me allowed another to do what he wanted unless he wanted it. I would have to explain how I met him and they would all say it was my fault. I said no and that was all that mattered. NO meant NO!

The only person I felt comfortable talking to was Darrel. Darrel was the perfect man. Any woman or man would want to be with him. Close your eyes and picture Morris Chestnut. Darrel reminds me of him. He was my height but about ten pounds heavier. His broad smile together with the personality made for a devastating combination. I had met him while I was attending Knox Community College and had noticed that he had eyes on me but I was never interested in him like that. We later got acquainted at the University of the West Indies where he pursued me even more vigorously. I was so scared to talk to him as it was alleged on campus that he was gay and by talking to him it would cramp my style and I couldn't allow that. He finished school a semester before me and even though he left the island we still kept in contact.

The day I told Darrel that I was raped was the day I was about to take a pill overdose. I had to, I just needed the pain and guilt I felt within to go away and only death could ease the pain I felt. I had failed myself and once more allowed someone to take my soul away. I cried in Darrel arms. He hugged me close to him and told me that it would all be OK. He held me so tight I never wanted him to let go off me. It was the first time in my life I cried so much and I felt my pain go away with each tear that fell. I cried aloud and it felt great, and I never felt embarrassed at how he was going to look at me or how he felt about me. I was still a man and something within me told me he understood what I was going through. He wiped the tears and he held me even tighter as we lay in my bed. It was the first time in my life I felt the true meaning of a hug and what it can do to a hurting person. At this point I yearned for the father I never had, that strong male figure, who should have been there to protect me, to shield me all these years. My anger at that moment grew towards my mother. I realized from an early age that she was not there for me. She could have hugged me but she was too consumed with her own life to even care. Darrel and I lay in silence for a long time. I never wanted him to go.

It took Darrel five years to get this close to me. I remember Darrel rubbing my head when he told me to look into his eyes. He saw my pain and I knew he loved me, not just that day, but five years ago when he saw me at Knox College. He told me that I was not alone, and that an uncle of his raped him, as well. He never gave me much detail but he told me that it was for him to deal with it. Like so many others like him, he has not dealt with it and may never do so. He was never wanted the memories to come back and I believed it would kill him if it did. Its locked up in the back of his mind and he is hoping that it never comes out. Darrel spent the two days before I left Jamaica with me at my home in the country and I will treasure those memories until I die. I had forgiven him for not being more persistent in an effort to woo me, but I think it was meant to be. He now resides in the US and we still keep in contact with each other.

Being gay, bi or whatever some people may call it, I don't know if my desire for men is as a result of my absentee father or the fact that I was sexually abused as a child. Now that I have my father in my life I have a high expectation of his role. Regrettably he has failed thus far but I have forgiven him just the same. There is still a strong yearning for men. There is a sense of protection, love and comfort from a man that I desire most. I also yearn for the love, affection and attention that my mother never gave to me. In truth, I can find comfort from both a man and a woman. I love both my parents and it's a gift to know them both, as many children have no clue who their parents are. I do hope the day will come when they will open their arms and be parents. Love isn't material possession. Parents it is important to say the word 'love' to your children, let them know that you love them. No matter how many expensive top of the line brand name clothing you buy for your children it will never compensate for you saying to them that you love them. The word is all that matters.

New York City was my only hope. It was my dream. E. Lynn Harris had enticed me with the city that never sleeps. He engulfed my mind with his character of Basil Henderson, how he used sex to ease his pain and anger. Basil and I could relate in so many ways, and it was his character that convinced me that New York was the place to be. I wanted to live a decent life. I wanted new friends and I wanted to go to the Nickel bar, get drunk and f—-k. I wanted the bond of friends and yes I did find it in this sometimes-lonely city. Winters were my worst. My newfound hobbies were shopping and sex. Each time I was angry or upset, I would go out and find a new partner or shop my ass off. I was in debt up to my neck and many times I felt like selling myself but, I knew I could not live with myself if I did. With all that I have been through I have now come to realize that I have a weakness for men. Sometimes I try to force myself to think that I like them, especially the ones that I have f——ked but when I think about it I hate them all. It has always been a challenge of mine to f——k the more masculine looking men as it was more of a conquest and f——king them gave me an imaginary power over them. The number of men I have f——ked out of anger and as a means to get over my own selfish guilt of rape are countless. At age twenty-four I have lessened my sexual encounters with both men and women as I now realize that I am addicted to sex and if I continue I would self-destruct. I used to shop to ease my pain and I am now in debt for over $15,000.00. Each time I would walk out of a store with the shopping bags it made me feel good but the saddest thing was by the time I got home the problems were still there. I am no longer a compulsive shopper and I am happy for that; however I still do believe that I must look sophisticated.

My life took a turn when my best friend from home who was living with me started to give me the cold shoulder and avoided me. He was scared that I was gay and someone had convinced him that I was in love with him, as I was too dependent on him. Yes I was dependent on him as he was all I had but I was never in love with him. He was the last person on earth I had expected to reject me. I thought he understood me and he was a friend. It happened at a time when I was evicted from my apartment, I had just finished my 1st degree. (I had failed my final year because of the rape and had to complete school in the US). I had no job and I had bills to pay. To me it seems as if he never cared. I felt trapped, I lost weight and I moved from 135lb to 112lb in less than one week. I could not eat and I vomited constantly. God put a stop to all this madness when one day I fainted on Flatbush Avenue and I had to be rushed to Kings County Hospital. I felt that it was just a pain but the doctors rushed me to the emergency room and wanted to operate on me immediately as I was bleeding internally. I refused to give them permission to cut me, so they did as much testing as they could, taking blood and came up with nothing. I was convinced that I had HIV, as they refused to say anything to me and one nurse asked me about my sexual history. I was now fighting not only for love but also for survival. I knew then that I had to clean my soul and my heart.

I was still losing weight. On the third day in the hospital I still could not eat and the diarrhea never stopped. On that night with all the pain I felt with the tubes in my arms and in my nostrils, I went on my knees and I spoke to God. This time I wasn't asking questions, I never needed answers, I just wanted him to forgive me. I wanted it all to end. I had to make a change and I realized that the change could only come from within. I asked God to allow me the strength to forgive myself. On a late night of June 2002, I forgave them, all the men who took advantage of me. I had to forgive them in order to move on with my life. That night I felt a peace of mind I had never felt in my life and though it was a strange feeling I knew it was over. The next day, I was able to eat, by midday I took a chance at walking and I did it with strength and vigor. I then realized the power of forgiveness, I will live with the memories of what these men did to me for the rest of my life but if I never forgave them I could not have continued with my life. On the fifth day, the day I walked out of the hospital. I made a plan. I wrote it down. I was going to start my life over, and close the chapters of my life that was filled with pain anger and abuse, it wasn't easy but I had to try.

Honestly I tried but once more I failed. I failed miserably at trying to change my life. I had stopped drinking and I had regained my weight but I still had mad issues to deal with. I wanted someone to love me, someone to hold me in their arms; I wasn't looking for a man or a woman, just someone who could hold me. It would have taken a beast if it could hold me and love me. I needed most of all cry and I needed to cry from deep within my soul and let the pain and anger out, but I was scared to do it on my own. I yearned for my grandma, I never accepted the reality that she was dead and I had to let go of her. I would go out late at nights in search for sex, where I use to live in Bedford-Stuyvesant in Brooklyn, and it was so easy to find sex. I remembered it was raining one night and I picked this guy up from the corner of my block and I f__ked the hell out of him. I never saw him again, I don't even remember what he looked like, I just wanted sex, and I wanted it then and there. It was as if I was taking out my anger on him and in fact that was exactly what I was doing, I was punishing him as if he was my abusers.

I found a new love for sex. I had created a façade, I never wanted to face the world I lived in, and so I used sex as a means to rid myself of the pain and hurt. I honestly felt then that sex was love because at times men can say the right words to you just when you want to hear them, but all they needed themselves is sex. The few minutes of sex gave me comfort and it did ease my pain. Well just for that moment. I never wanted a commitment. It was all about sex and more sex. I would marvel myself at how good I was at it. On a typical day I could have had sex with five different men. By the end of the week, I could have been with over twenty different men. Yes I did use protection, durex was my best friend.

I was very aware of HIV and AIDS and at one point I even felt that I was infected with the virus, but I didn't gave a f__k about living any more. I wanted a quick way out of life. I was scared to commit suicide so this would kill me slowly. I never enjoyed going to clubs then, I hated the idea of two men dancing together, it made me sick, I never wanted to mix with the gay crowd. In my eyes I was far from being gay. I always had a thing for straight acting men, as they felt that they were more man than I was, and what I had was enough weapon to hold him calm and I used it well. I was young and full of energy and I could go for long. I have a strong hatred for bi-sexual men or those on the down low as they reminded me too much of my abusers and I would fuck these men with so much anger they would beg me to stop.

The sex lessened in the middle of writing this book, when I had re-read my journals and I then realized what I was doing to myself. I was now living in Westchester and it was quite difficult finding a man as I was too far from the action. Even though I would travel to Brooklyn occasionally I would return home drained and unable to write. The night I wrote the first rape scene it shuck me up and then I realized that sex was the root to all of my problems and it sure could not be the solution. I realized that night that no matter how many times I had sex, the pain and anger remained just the same. I still do love sex, trust me I do, but I no longer do it just for having sex. I try to get to know the person for who they are first, it's a new and odd feeling but it's the safest way to go. I had a reality check when I went to visit a friend and I found out that he was dying from HIV and there was nothing that I could do for him. We had similar issues and he used sex as a means to rid himself of the pain. It was sad seeing him there, looking lifeless and he never wanted to get help as he felt that only death could ease his pain. I then became sacred of HIV and most importantly I was scared of dying. I know what I had to do but I was scared.

I eventually took the test and it came back negative. I can still remember my friends face and he was still in pain and it's so sad that his life had to end this way. He was full of energy and he had mad jokes. He wanted us to be together but it could never happen as I had too much on my plate. He still does not believe that he is gay and even in death I could still see his joy and him searching for love. His family never believed him when he told them that he was raped and it killed his soul. This book is for him and that seven-year-old boy who killed himself. There are countless other cases and voices that need to be heard. I have now open up the wounds that so many men think that was healed. On the outside the scars may have disappeared but deep within, it is far from healing. This book is just not for me, it's for all of us, and you are not alone. Too many souls have been lost and the strength comes only from wit in. It is not easy I know, but we will have to deal with the past at some point in time and there is no better time than the present.

I have now started loving me more, taking longer walks, reading more enjoying plays and good company. In order to move on I had to drop some people out of my life who had negative energies. If you hang around people with negative energies, it will become a part of you. Positive attract positive energies and that is all I need around me. I have forgiven my family for turning their backs on me. I opened my arms wide to my mother in an attempt to understand her way of thinking. If she never said I love you ever, I love me now and it no longer matters. I love my mother and I will always love her unconditionally. Life isn't a bed of roses; good things happen to those who wait. If life was handed down to me on a platter I may not have valued it so much. I no longer take life for granted. Everything that happened to me, I take it as an experience and I try to take the good out of each situation. Things happen in life for a reason.

Each night I go to bed I reflect on the day. I wake up each day not just for me but for my younger sister. I have so much love and affection for her. I now have regrets for how I treated her as a child, but I had instilled some core values in her and that is self worth, the value of education and the openness to express herself so that if she ever got molested she would have the courage and the willingness to speak up about it. I gave her that power, and that is the power of choice to speak up and not hide. I have grown to love her even more now, and it is her who keeps me alive. Barbara Walters in an interview with Oprah for O Magazine, October 2004 issue said 'you have got to have someone you love—and not necessarily that you have to have someone who love you. You've got to have a reason to get up in the morning...But you must have something you really care about. And you must have friends." Barbara could not have put it better. My friends are my world, they have endured my attitudes, hold me when I needed someone to cry with me, they have had my back in both good and bad times. They have even called me black Martha. I thank the five men in my life for their unconditional love and support and if it was not for them this book could not have been written. They have taught me the art of forgiveness and how to love again and I dedicate this chapter to them.

Forgiveness is the key to the healing process. As a survivor of sexual abuse, you must forgive yourself for not knowing how to protect yourself. You must forgive yourself for needing and wanting to take the time to heal. And you must give yourself all the kindness, compassion and love you can. Direct all your attention and your energies towards your own living and survival. The ultimate goal is to be happy and realize that what happened to you wasn't your fault.

My life's journey is far from coming to an end, but at this point in my life I am happy and at peace with myself. I am happy because I have made the choice to be happy, I have made my peace with God and he has forgiven me. I don't know if I will publish this book or what will become of it, who knows. I can say one thing for sure, writing this book was a challenge and it was the best thing I have ever attempted to do in my life. It was a healing process, I have shed some of my tears and now I have moved on. I am still looking for that someone to hold me when I cry. I encourage all victims who have been molested to find themselves, to first forgive themselves and those who have hurt them and move on. I am older, wiser and stronger now and I hope the light within me can reflect to the world the changes I have made and the man I have become. It is the end of summer 2004 and I am still searching for a love of my own, someone to love me for me, to hold me, listen to my fears, someone who will not judge me based on my past. One thing for sure I am happy and that is all that matters now. I have been through so much, accomplished so much with little or nothing at all; I can now face the world with nothing.

This is the beginning of a journey. The men represented in the book are all educated men; I decided to relay the stories of only those men who have used education as a means of escape from all the hurt and turmoil they were faced with. Some have fess up and decided to get professional help while some are still trying to garner the courage to face the past and rid themselves of the guilt that it was their fault. Nonetheless they are all brave men, brave to have started the process and brave to have opened up and trusted me with their stories. The most important thing is that I have taught them how to forgive and to realize that it was never their fault. I hope that as a result of dealing with their past those around them may be able to see the change within them. I started with the creation story and now I end with how our work on earth should be done.

St. Matthew 5:16
Let your light shine before men, that they may see your good works, and glorify your father, which is in heaven,

Resources

✦

Help for Survivors

Jamaica

Victims Support Unit
Head Office
47 East Old Hope Road
Kingston #5
Jamaica W.I
(876) 946-0663

The Center for Investigation of sexual Offences and Child Abuse
C.I.S.O.C.A
Community Relations Branch of
The Jamaica Constabulary Force
Head Quarters
3 Ruthven Rd.
Kingston 10
www.jamaicapolice.org.jm

Jamaica Forum for Lesbians
All Sexual and Gays J-FLAG
P.O. Box 1152
Kingston 8
Jamaica W.I
(876) 978-8988
www.jflag.org

United States

National Gay & Lesbian Task Force
2320 17th Street, NW

Washington, DC 20009
(202) 332-6483

Survivors of Incest Anonymous
World Service Office, P.O. Box 190
Bengon, MD 21018-9998
(410) 893-3322
www.siawso.org

Rape, Abuse & Incest National Network
635B Pennsylvania Avenue SE
Washington, DC 20003
(203) 544-1034 Ext. 1
www.roinn.org

MaleSurvivors
PMB103
5505 Connecticut Avenue, NW
Washington, DC 20015-2601
www.maleSurvivors.org

National Coalition Against Sexual Assault
125 N. Enola Drive
(717) 728-9764

Men's Resource Center
12 Southeast 14th
Portland, OR 97214
(503) 235-3433

Free Referral List

Nationwide

RAINN (Rape, Abuse, and Incest National Network)
Referral to rape crisis programs and services nationwide
1-800-656-HOPE

New York

Safe Horizon Victim Services Agency
Offices throughout NYC
212-577-7777

LifeNet, NYC Dep. Of Health and Mental Hygiene
Crisis intervention and referral hotline
1-800-LIFENET

Brooklyn

Rape Crisis Intervention and Victim of Violence
Program at Long Island College Hospital
718-780-1459

Jewish Board of Family Children Services
718-237-1337

Manhattan

Mount Sinai SAVI
(Sexual Assault and Violence Intervention) Program
212-423-2140

St. Luke's Roosevelt Crime Treatment Center
212-523-4728

St. Vincent's Hospital
212-604-8068

Queens

Mount Sinai SAVI
(Sexual Assault and Violence Intervention) Program
718-736-1288

New Jersey

Bergen

YWCA of Bergen County Rape Crisis Center
201-487-2227

Essex

UMDNJ (University of Medicine and Dentistry of New Jersey)
Safe and Sound Rape Care Program
973-972-1324

Hudson

Christ Hospital Mental Health Center
201-795-8375

Morris

Health and Counseling Sexual Assault Services
973-829-0581

Passaic

Passaic County Center
973-881-1450

Canada

MaleSurvivors
c/o BCSMSSA
1252 Burrard St., #202
Vancouver, B.C
V6Z1

United Kingdom

Mankind UK—Support/Resources
www.mankinduk.co.uk

Male Rape Support Association
24 hour help-line 07932 898274
www.malereapesexualabuse.ik.com
E-mail: malerapemrsa@yahoo.co.uk

Maleabuse.org
A UK site that supports male survivors of sexual abuse
www.maleabuse.org

Breaking Free
Suite 21-25 Marshall House
124 Middleton Road
Morden
Surrey
SM4 6RW
(020) 8648-3500

2nd Floor
Clayton Chambers
59-61 Westgate Road
Newcastle-UPON-TYNE
Ne1 5SG
0191 221 1919
Monday to Friday 10am to 6pm
E-mail ASCANorthEast2aol.com

4 Rose Hill
Chesterfield
S40 1LW
01246 234 234
E-mail cm.survivors@btinternet.com

Luton and Districts Rape Crisis Center
12 Oxford Road
Luton
LUI 3AX
Mon—Thurs. 10am-4pm
Office: 01582 733592
Helpline: 01582 733592

Help for offenders

STOP IT NOW

P.O. Box 495
Hoydenville, MA 01039
(888) Prevent; (888-773-8368)
www.stopitnow.org

Books

These are works of nonfiction and fiction that I have read and from which I have garnered information. There are noted books and articles on this list that I strongly recommend survivors of child abuse read:

Angelou, Maya. *I Know the Caged Bird Sing*. Bantam, New York, 1983

Bass, Ellen and Davis, Laura. *Beginning to Heal: A First Book for Survivors of Child Sexual Abuse*. Harper Perennial, 1993

Dugan, Meg Kennedy, and Roger Hock. *It's My Life Now: Starting Over after an Abusive Relationship or Domestice Violence*. Routledge, New York, 2000.

Fisher, Antwone Q. *Finding Fish*. Harper Torch, New York, 2002

Gerdes, Louise I. *Child Abuse: Opposing View Points Series*, Greenhaven Press, 2003

Lew, Mike. *Victims No Longer: Men Recovering from Incest and other Sexual Child Abuse*. Harper and Row Publishers, New York, 1990

Maltz, Wendy. *The Sexual Healing Journey: A Guide for Survivors of Sexual Abuse*. Harper Collins Publishers, 1991

Morrison, Toni. *Love*. Alfred A. Knopf, New York, 2003

Morrison, Toni. *The Bluest Eye*. Plume, New York, 1994

Robinson, Lori S. *I Will Survive: The African-American Guide to Healing from Sexual Assault and Abuse*. Seal press, New York, 2002

Sapphire. *Push*. Vintage Books, New York, 1997.

Scarce, Michael. *Male on Male rape: The Hidden Toll of Stigma and Shame*. Perseus Books. 1991

Stone, Robin D. *No Secrets No Lies: How Black Families Can Heal from Sexual Abuse*. Broadway Books, New York, 2004

Walker, Alice. *The Color Purple*. Harcourt Brace Jovanovich, New York, 1982

Bibliography

Baker, Christopher P. *Jamaica: In-depth Full-color Reggae Section.* Loney Planet Publications. 2nd ed. 2000

Bass, Elen, and Davis, Laura *Beginning to Heal: A first Book for Men and Women who were Sexually abused as children.* HarperCollins Publishers, Inc. New York, NY, 1993

Bradley, Lloy *This is Reggae Music: The Story of Jamaica Music.* Grave Press, New York. 2000

Cossins, Ann *Masculinities, Sexualities and Child Sexual Abuse.* Klumer Law International, The Hague, The Netherlands, 2000

Edge, Kim. *The Sexual Assault of Men and Boys: Men and Boys as Victims.* Rape Victim Advocacy Program, University of Iowa

Euquene, Patron J. *Heart of Lavender: In Search of Gay Africa.* Harvard Gay & Lesbian Review, Harvard, Fall 1995

Finkelhor, David. *A Source Book on Child Sexual Abuse.* Beverly Hills, Sage Publication, 1986

Finklhor, David. *Early and Long-Term Effects of Child Sexual Abuse: An Update.* Family Research, Laboratory, University of New Hampshire. 1986

Gartner, Richard, Phd. *Myths About Male Sexual Victimization.* www.malesurvivor.org, 16 Feb. 2004

Garner, Bryan A. *Black Law Dictionary.* 7th ed. Editor. St. Paul. 1999

Gerdes, Louise I. *Child Abuse: Opposing View Points Series.* Greenhaven Press. 2003

Hopper, Jim, Phd. *Sexual Abuse of Males, Prevalence, Possible lasting effects and resources.* www.jimhopper.com 18 Nov. 2003

Hunter, Tierney E. *Men Don't Cry,* Essence Magazine, March, 2003

Hurston, Zora. *Tell My Horse: Voodoo and life in Haiti and Jamaica.* Harper & Row Publishers, New York, 1938

King J.L. *On the Down Low.* Broadway. April, 2004

Kenneth, Adams M. *Silently Seduced: When Parents Make their Children Partners, Understanding covert Incest.* Health Communications, INC. Florida, 1991

Lew, Mike *Victims No longer: Men Recovering from Incest and Other Sexual Child Abuse.* Harper & Row Publishers, New York, 1986

Maltz, Wendy. *The Sexual Healing Journey: A Guide for Survivors of Sexual Abuse.* Harper Collins Publishers, 1991

McMullen, Richie J. *Male Rape: Breaking The Silence On The Last Taboo.* Alyson Publications, 1990

Michel, Dorois *Don't Tell: The Sexual Abuse of Boys.* Queens University Press, 2002

Moore, Daryl T. *Breaking the Cane.* Essence Magazine, April 2003

Murray, Stephen O. *Boy-Wives and Female-Husbands: Studies of African Homosexuality.* PALEGAVE, New York, 1998

Pryor, Douglas W. *Unspeakable Acts; Why Men Sexually abuse Children.* New York University Press, New York, 1996

Scarce, Michael. *Male on Male Rape: The Hidden Toll of Stigma and Shame.* Insight Books/Plenumm, New York, 1997

Simms-Constantine, Delroy. *The Greatest Taboo: Homosexuality in Black Communities.* Ed. Henry Louis Gates Jr. Alyson Publications, California, 20001

Stone, Robin D. *No Secret No Lies: How Black Families can Heal from Sexual Abuse.* Broadway Books, New York, 2004

Stella Orakwue. *History Most Sordid Cover Up.* New Africa. No.426. Feb. 2004

Tara, Ney, Phd. *True and False Allegations of Child Sexual Abuse Assessment and Case Management.* Brunner. Mazel, Inc. New York 1995

Wildman, Noah. *So You want to be a Rude Boy?* The People's Ska Annual. Issue #4